Focusing on IELTS

General Training
Practice Tests

Focusing on IELTS

General Training Practice Tests

Second edition

MACMILLAN

Michael Clutterbuck
Philip Gould

First edition published 2005 by the National Centre for English Language Teaching and Research,
Macquarie University (reprinted once)
Second edition published 2011 by
MACMILLAN EDUCATION AUSTRALIA PTY LTD
15–19 Claremont Street, South Yarra 3141

Associated companies and representatives
throughout the world.

National Library of Australia
cataloguing in publication data

Author:	Clutterbuck, Michael
Title:	Focusing on IELTS: General Training Practice Tests / Michael Clutterbuck, Philip Gould.
Edition:	2nd ed.
ISBN:	978 1 4202 3021 5 (pbk.)
Subjects:	International English Language Testing System.
	English language—Study and teaching—Foreign speakers.
	English language—Examinations.
Other authors/contributors:	Gould, Philip, 1959–
Dewey number:	428.0076

Publisher: Vivienne Winter
Project editors: Kirstie Innes-Will and Laura Howell
Editor: Ingrid De Baets
Cover and text designer: Anne Stanhope
Photo research and permissions clearance: Jes Senbergs
Typeset in 11.5 pt Sabon by Marg Jackson, Emtype Desktop Publishing
Cover image: Shutterstock

Printed in China

Contents

How to use this book

There are no magic formulas or secret keys that guarantee a good score in the IELTS test. The best way to prepare for the exam is to gradually improve your overall English listening, reading, writing and speaking abilities.

It is useful to train for the kinds of texts and questions you will face in the IELTS exam. *Focusing on IELTS: General Training Practice Tests* contains complete Reading, Writing, Listening and Speaking practice tests for you to try out. Each test in this book is identical in format to the General Training IELTS tests themselves. You should work through these under test conditions, which means working in a room where you won't be disturbed and only spending an hour on each Reading and Writing Test. There are sample answer sheets at the end of the Listening and Reading units for you to photocopy and use each time you do a practice Listening or Reading Test. This book also contains three recorded sample Speaking Tests for you to listen to. You can read the transcripts of these Sample Tests, along with an analysis of each of the three candidates' performances. At the back of the book, there are transcripts for the Listening Tests and an answer key for the Listening and Reading Tests. There are sample answers for the Writing Tests.

You can use this book individually as an independent study guide to prepare for the General Training IELTS test or as practice materials for an IELTS preparation course with a teacher.

You may also want to work more intensively on the skills needed in the different sections of the test. For this reason *Focusing on IELTS: General Training Practice Tests* has been written to accompany *Focusing on IELTS: Reading and Writing Skills* by Jeremy Lindeck, Jannette Greenwood and Kerry O'Sullivan (Macmillan 2011) and *Focusing on IELTS: Listening and Speaking Skills* by Steven Thurlow and Kerry O'Sullivan (Macmillan 2011). These two books thoroughly examine the skills you need and teach useful strategies to help you perform well in the test.

Acknowledgments

Author acknowledgments

I am grateful for the friendly support I have received from Vivienne Winter at Macmillan, and also for the helpful advice and recommendations from Anna Dash, Kate Chandler and Philip Gould. Ingrid De Baets also made valuable suggestions, and I would like particularly to acknowledge the expert and detailed guidance from Mary Jane Hogan.

Michael Clutterbuck

I would like to thank the following people for their help during the writing of this book: Anna Dash, Alison Babbage, Lisa Barrett, Penny Bell, Mary Cristaudo, Pauline Cullen, Dennis Derkenne, Mary Jane Hogan, Xiaojing Luo, Diana Montgomery and Hasan Can Yuksel. Thanks also to the students who helped with the trialling of these materials.

Philip Gould

Publisher acknowledgments

What is in the listening module?

This test is the same for Academic and General Training candidates.

Time allowed	Approximately 30 minutes, plus 10 minutes to transfer answers to answer sheet
Procedure	The listening module is the first part of the test you will do. The listening module is recorded using a range of accents of standard English. The recording is played once only. Candidates are given a question booklet. Time is given to read the questions before each section is heard. As you listen to the recording of each section, write your answers in the question booklet. At the end of the fourth section, you are given 10 minutes to transfer your answers to an answer sheet.
Number of questions	40 questions (10 questions per section) 1 mark per question
Structure of the test	**Section 1:** a conversation between two speakers in a normal life situation, e.g. buying a ticket **Section 2:** a monologue (i.e. spoken by one speaker) about a social (non-academic) topic, e.g. joining a club **Section 3:** a conversation between two to four speakers about an educational or training topic, e.g. what the students are studying **Section 4:** a presentation by one speaker in a situation related to educational or training contexts

Summary of the structure	Easier ↓ Harder	Section 1	Dialogue	Social topics
		Section 2	Monologue	
		Section 3	Dialogue	Education and training topics
		Section 4	Monologue	

Listening strategies and skills	See detailed guidelines in 'Listening strategies and skills', *Focusing on IELTS: Listening and Speaking Skills* (Thurlow and O'Sullivan 2011), pages 13–47.

Question types

The following question types are used in the listening module:

▼ *Multiple choice* – you have to choose one answer from three alternatives or two answers from five alternatives.

▼ *Short answer* – you have to answer a question. You will be given a maximum number of words and/or numbers for your answer.

▼ *Sentence completion* – you have to find words that correctly complete a sentence.

▼ *Form/note/summary/flow-chart/table completion* – you have to complete a form, set of notes, summary, flow-chart or table. You will be given a maximum number of words for your answer.

▼ *Labelling a diagram/plan/map* – you have to identify features of a diagram, plan or map.

▼ *Matching* – you have to choose answers from a box containing three, five, seven or nine possible answers.

For detailed explanation, see *Focusing on IELTS: Listening and Speaking Skills* (Thurlow and O'Sullivan 2011) pages 6–12.

Tips for doing the Listening Test

▼ Make sure you are familiar with each question type before you do the test so you know how to respond.

▼ Use the time given to read the questions before each section.

▼ Remember to look at all the sets of questions in each section, not just the first set.

▼ Follow the instructions exactly; for example, regarding the maximum number of words your response should have.

▼ Use the questions to identify the topic of each section and predict what vocabulary you might hear.

▼ Listen with attention to the overall topic so that what you hear makes sense.

▼ Anticipate the type of information needed to answer each question.

▼ Remember that you may hear synonyms and paraphrases of words and ideas in the questions.

▼ Be aware of the question following the one you are answering and move on if you hear the next answer.

▼ Stay focused on the test; don't be distracted or let your attention wander.

▼ If you miss a question, guess an answer in the time given to review your responses.

▼ Be very careful to copy your answers correctly onto the answer sheet.

▼ Be careful with spelling as incorrect spelling is penalised.

Listening Test 1

TIME ALLOWED: APPROXIMATELY 30 MINUTES, PLUS 10 MINUTES TO TRANSFER ANSWERS

NUMBER OF QUESTIONS: 40

This test has been written to simulate the IELTS test in its style, format, level of difficulty, question types and length. You should do this test under IELTS test conditions. This means playing the recording only once without pausing or stopping.

Instructions

You will hear four different recordings and you will have to answer questions on what you hear.

There will be time for you to read the instructions and questions before the recording is played. You will also have the opportunity to check your answers.

The recording will be played **ONCE** only.

The test is in four sections. Write your answers on the question sheet as you listen. At the end of Section 4 you have 10 minutes to transfer your answers onto the answer sheet, which is on page 31. When you finish, check the answer key at the back of the book.

Now turn to Section 1 on the next page.

SECTION 1

Questions 1–5

Complete the notes below.

*Write **NO MORE THAN THREE WORDS AND/OR A NUMBER** for each answer.*

Change of address	
Customer number:	Example: ...*5062 7840*...............................
Name:	1 ....
Date of birth:	2 ....
New address:	18 King Street, 3 ....
New telephone number:	4 ....
Billing period:	5 ....

Questions 6–10

*Choose the correct letter, **A**, **B** or **C**.*

6 The contract the customer has now is

    A Economy Saver.

    B Flexible Bundle.

    C Home Plus.

7 The contract the customer will have in the future is

    A Economy Saver.

    B Home Plus.

    C Three-In-One.

8 There are no limits on Internet downloads in the period from

    A 10 pm to 6 am.

    B 1 am to 6 am.

    C 11 pm to 2 am.

9 Most of the phone calls this customer makes are

    A to friends.

    B to relatives.

    C for work.

10 Overall, the customer finds that the service of the telephone company is

    A satisfactory.

    B excellent.

    C very good.

Complete the notes below.

Write **NO MORE THAN THREE WORDS AND/OR A NUMBER** *for each answer.*

▼   Always wear **11** .... inside the hotel.

▼   Hire beach items at the **12** ....

▼   Reception opening hours **13** ....

▼   Linen and towels are changed **14** ....

▼   Smoking allowed only **15** ....

▼   Do not feed the **16** .... and the ....

▼   Be quiet after **17** ....

Questions 18–20

*Choose **TWO** letters, A–E.*

18   Which TWO types of rubbish are *not* recycled?

    A   food scraps

    B   glass

    C   metal

    D   newspaper

    E   plastic

19   Which TWO types of facilities in the hotel do you have to pay to use?

    A   gym

    B   spa

    C   billiards

    D   Internet

    E   DVDs

20   What are TWO places for evening entertainment within walking distance of the hotel?

    A   bar

    B   casino

    C   cinema

    D   karaoke club

    E   nightclub

SECTION 3

Questions 21–30

Questions 21–26

When patients have the following problems, who does the nurse need to contact first?

*Choose your answers from the box and write the correct letters, **A–F**, next to questions 21–26.*

A confusion	**D** poor eyesight
B instability when walking	**E** refusal to accept help
C pets as a risk factor	**F** weakness

21   physiotherapist   ....

22   doctor   ....

23   occupational therapist   ....

24   aged care team   ....

25   dietitian   ....

26   falls clinic   ....

Questions 27–30

*Choose the correct letter, **A**, **B** or **C**.*

27   In which of the following medical problems can the damage be reversed?

    A   long-term, excessive alcohol consumption

    B   Pick's disease

    C   a brain tumour

28   Anxiety is a common symptom among people with dementia due to

    A   side effects of medication.

    B   frustration and suspicion.

    C   fear of the future.

29   People with dementia tend to enjoy food that is

    A   sweet.

    B   easy to chew.

    C   salty.

30   Recent research has shown people with dementia often benefit from

    A   singing.

    B   listening to music.

    C   exercise.

*Write **NO MORE THAN TWO WORDS AND/OR A NUMBER** for each answer.*

The Tuareg

▼ Difficult to count Tuareg population due to **31** ………………..……………… .

▼ Tuareg people's skin often looks blue because of colour of their **32** ………………..……………. .

Diet

▼ Dry season: grains and fruit.

▼ Wet season: **33** ………………..……………. and ………………..……………… .

Occupations of Tuareg in countryside

▼ Breeding animals.

▼ Trade and **34** ………………..……………… .

Camel caravans

▼ For trade between Sahel and Mediterranean.

▼ Maximum load per camel: 300 kilograms plus rider.

▼ Travel south slowly at first so camels can **35** ………………..……………… .

Trade partners

▼ Hausa people trade cloth and millet for **36** ………………..……………… and dates.

Questions 37–40

Choose the correct letter, A, B or C.

37   The main work of Tuareg women in growing crops is

    A   planting.

    B   irrigating.

    C   harvesting.

38   Tuareg women mainly look after

    A   camels and cattle.

    B   cattle and sheep.

    C   goats and donkeys.

39   Salt prices are highest in the hotter weather because at that time of year

    A   animals need more salt.

    B   the quality of the salt is best.

    C   transport by camel is more difficult.

40   Craftsmen had low status in traditional Tuareg society because

    A   they did not work as farmers.

    B   they did not live as nomads.

    C   they had a different attitude to education.

Listening Test 2

TIME ALLOWED: APPROXIMATELY 30 MINUTES, PLUS 10 MINUTES TO TRANSFER ANSWERS

NUMBER OF QUESTIONS: 40

This test has been written to simulate the IELTS test in its style, format, level of difficulty, question types and length. You should do this test under IELTS test conditions. This means playing the recording only once without pausing or stopping.

Instructions

You will hear four different recordings and you will have to answer questions on what you hear.

There will be time for you to read the instructions and questions before the recording is played. You will also have the opportunity to check your answers.

The recording will be played **ONCE** only.

The test is in four sections. Write your answers on the question sheet as you listen. At the end of Section 4 you have 10 minutes to transfer your answers onto the answer sheet, which is on page 31. When you finish, check the answer key at the back of the book.

Now turn to Section 1 on the next page.

SECTION 1

Questions 1–5

Complete the notes below.

*Write **NO MORE THAN TWO WORDS AND/OR A NUMBER** for each answer.*

Application for driving licence	
Name:	Example: ....*Theresa Collins*..........................
Class of licence:	1 ....
Date of birth:	17 March 1994
Address:	2 .... Street, Bentley
Phone number:	3 ....
Identification:	4 ....
Method of payment:	5 ....

Questions 6–10

*Choose the correct letter, **A**, **B** or **C**.*

6 In the test of road rules, you are allowed to make no more than

    A one mistake.

    B two mistakes.

    C four mistakes.

7 A person who has a learner's licence can only drive with a person

    A who has a provisional licence.

    B who has a full licence.

    C who is an authorised driving instructor.

8 A provisional licence is valid for

    A 9 months.

    B 18 months.

    C 6 months.

9 The maximum speed for a person who has a learner's licence is

    A 60 km per hour.

    B 100 km per hour.

    C 80 km per hour.

10 While driving, a person is

    A not allowed to use a mobile phone.

    B only allowed to use a mobile phone if they are not holding it.

    C allowed to send an SMS.

SECTION 2

Questions 11–15

What is stated about the following means of transport from the airport?

*Choose your answers from the box below and write the correct letters, **A–G**, next to questions 11–15.*

A cheapest		**E** most popular	
B fastest		**F** most reliable	
C most comfortable		**G** safest	
D most environmentally friendly			

11 trains ....

12 minibuses ....

13 buses ....

14 cars ....

15 taxis ....

Questions 16–20

Label the floor plan below.

*Choose **FIVE** answers from the box below and write the correct letters, **A–H**, next to numbers 16–20 on the floor plan.*

A cafe	**E** pharmacy
B dress shop	**F** smoking room
C Internet cafe	**G** toilets
D newsagency	**H** wine bar

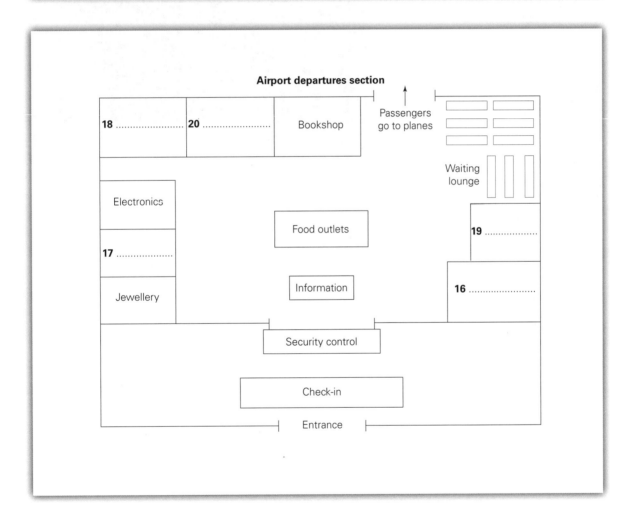

Questions 21–26

CD 1 • Track 9 *Choose the correct letter, **A**, **B** or **C**.*

21 The largest numbers of Tasmanian devils live in

  A   coastal areas.

  B   drier forests.

  C   rainforests.

22 An adult female can weigh up to

  A   4.5 kg.

  B   9 kg.

  C   13 kg.

23 Tasmanian devils are

  A   shy.

  B   aggressive.

  C   friendly.

24 In one year an adult female usually raises

  A   one baby.

  B   three babies.

  C   twenty babies.

25 Tasmanian devils become independent when they are about

  A   5 months old.

  B   8 months old.

  C   2 years old.

26 Farmers are

  A   permitted to shoot or poison them.

  B   paid to kill them.

  C   prohibited from killing them.

Questions 27–30

Complete the summary below using words from the box.

*Choose **FOUR** answers from the box and write the correct letters, **A–I**, next to questions 27–30.*

A bark	**F** friendly
B bite	**G** sick
C clean	**H** yawn
D dead	**I** young
E fight	

Tasmanian devils live alone and move slowly. They usually eat **27** .... animals and

are not affected by the diseases of the animals they eat. They are generally **28** ....

They travel long distances at night and are famous for their strong appetite. To decide the order

in which they eat, Tasmanian devils often **29** .... , whereas if they are afraid, they

30 ....

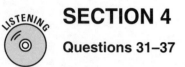

Questions 31–37

CD 1 • Track 10 *Complete the notes below.*

*Write **NO MORE THAN TWO WORDS AND/OR A NUMBER** for each answer.*

Framework of survey

▼   Aims of survey: investigate type of people who do yoga, styles of yoga, frequency of

       practice, **31** ……………..……………… for practice, benefits of yoga.

▼   Conducted via Internet due to effectiveness and **32** ………………..……………….. .

▼   4,000 respondents nationwide.

▼   Respondents: one-third teachers, two-thirds students, **33** ……………..…….……… women.

Findings of survey

▼   Males and younger people prefer more vigorous styles.

▼   Uses of yoga: **34** ………………..……………. and ………………..……………. , meditation,

       spiritual path.

▼   Approximately 2% of total population practise yoga; highest participation 35- to

       44-year-olds.

▼   Less time spent on physical exercise due to rise in popularity of **35** …………………..……….. .

▼   56% of yoga students do yoga one to two times per week; 56% of yoga teachers do yoga

       five to seven times per week.

▼   Reasons for starting yoga practice: health and fitness, **36** ……………..……………. , treat

       physical problem.

▼   Major motivation to continue yoga: **37** ……………..……………. .

Questions 38–40

*Choose the correct letter, **A**, **B** or **C**.*

38 A major cause of injuries when doing yoga is

    A headstand and shoulder stand.

    B students causing injuries to themselves.

    C teachers pushing students too hard.

39 A typical yoga teacher earns money

    A only from teaching yoga.

    B from massage therapy.

    C from nursing.

40 The speaker concludes that

    A teaching yoga is not a good way to earn a high income.

    B yoga is a relatively expensive form of exercise.

    C the benefits of yoga are uproven.

Listening Test 3

TIME ALLOWED: APPROXIMATELY 30 MINUTES, PLUS 10 MINUTES TO TRANSFER ANSWERS

NUMBER OF QUESTIONS: 40

This test has been written to simulate the IELTS test in its style, format, level of difficulty, question types and length. You should do this test under IELTS test conditions. This means playing the recording only once without pausing or stopping.

Instructions

You will hear four different recordings and you will have to answer questions on what you hear.

There will be time for you to read the instructions and questions before the recording is played. You will also have the opportunity to check your answers.

The recording will be played **ONCE** only.

The test is in four sections. Write your answers on the question sheet as you listen. At the end of Section 4 you have 10 minutes to transfer your answers onto the answer sheet, which is on page 31. When you finish, check the answer key at the back of the book.

Now turn to Section 1 on the next page.

SECTION 1

Questions 1–4

Complete the notes below.

Write **NO MORE THAN TWO WORDS AND/OR A NUMBER** *for each answer.*

Details of job applicant	
Name of applicant:	George Peters
Phone number:	Example: **0438 637 935**
Position applied for:	**1** ....
Previous work experience:	worked as a **2** ....
Qualifications:	currently studying **3** ....
Foreign languages spoken:	**4** .... and ....

Questions 5–7

Which duties are part of the job that the man is applying for?

*Choose **THREE** from the list below and write the correct letters, **A–G**, next to questions 5–7.*

A change light bulbs	**E** take food orders
B clear away plates	**F** take luggage to rooms
C deliver morning papers	**G** work in hotel bar
D stock refrigerators	

5 ....

6 ....

7 ....

Questions 8–10

Which of the following are provided for staff by the hotel?

*Choose **THREE** from the list below and write the correct letters, **A–G**, next to questions 8–10.*

A laundry	**E** training
B meals	**F** transport costs
C medical insurance	**G** uniforms
D parking	

8 ....

9 ....

10 ....

SECTION 2   Questions 11–20

Questions 11–12

*Choose **TWO** correct letters, A–E.*

11 Which TWO types of visa does the Atwood Immigration office handle?

A employment

B medical

C resident

D student

E tourist

12 Which TWO matters do students have to tell the Immigration Department about?

A change of address

B change of college

C holidays

D marriage

E work

Questions 13–20

Complete the notes in the flow-chart below.

*Write **NO MORE THAN THREE WORDS AND/OR A NUMBER** for each answer.*

How to extend a student visa

Pay for new course for a minimum period of **13** ……………..………………… .

↓

Letter from college stating that you attended at least **14** …………….…………… of previous classes.

↓

Get Form 726C from Immigration: from office or **15** ……………..…………… .

↓

Bank statement showing minimum bank balance of **16** ……………..…………… .

↓

Three **17** ……………..…………… .

↓

Take all documents and passport to Dept of Immigration at least three weeks before expiry of visa.

↓

Pay **18** ……………..…………… to extend visa.

↓

Wait twelve **19** ……………..…………… for reply.

↓

Might need to have an **20** ……………..…………… .

Questions 21–24

CD 2 • Track 4 *Choose the correct letter, A, B or C.*

21 The annual value of the beauty industry worldwide is

    A $15 billion.

    B $38 billion.

    C $160 billion.

22 The annual growth rate of the global beauty market is

    A   7%.

    B   14%.

    C   40%.

23 The most common form of cosmetic procedure is for

    A   fat.

    B   wrinkles.

    C   teeth.

24 Demand for beauty products increased in the early 20th century due to

    A   packaging.

    B   scientific progress.

    C   photography.

Questions 25–30

Who agrees with the following opinions?

Choose your answers from the box and write the correct letters, A–C, next to questions 25–30.

You may use any answer more than once.

> **A** Maggie (the female student)
> **B** Mike (the male student)
> **C** Maggie and Mike (both students)

25 50% of the money used for marketing is used effectively. ....

26 The beauty industry is based on hope and fear. ....

27 People who are more attractive earn higher incomes. ....

28 Attractive people tend not to accept poor treatment. ....

29 Clear skin is seen as a sign of women's youth and health. ....

30 The current beauty industry promotes fitness. ....

SECTION 4   Questions 31–40

Questions 31–35

Which of the following sources gave scientists information about the Iceman?

*Choose your answers from the box and write the correct letters, **A–H**, next to questions 31–35.*

A back	**C** fingernail	**E** intestines	**G** stomach
B bones	**D** hair	**F** skin	**H** teeth

31   age when he died   ....

32   where he lived   ....

33   food normally eaten   ....

34   health   ....

35   time of year when he died ....

Questions 36–40

*Choose the correct letter, **A**, **B** or **C**.*

36   Moss was used in the Iceman's region

    A   to wrap food.

    B   as toilet paper.

    C   to cook food.

37   His shoes were made from

    A   grass and bark.

    B   deer hide and goat hide.

    C   bearskin and goatskin.

38   It is most likely that the Iceman was a

    A   shepherd.

    B   hunter.

    C   trader.

39   It is now believed the Iceman died

    A   near the rock where his body was found.

    B   while trapped under a rock.

    C   while sleeping on the rock where his body was found.

40   Much evidence was destroyed

    A   due to the manner in which he died and the isolated location of his corpse.

    B   because people initially didn't realise the importance of the discovery.

    C   when the autopsy was carried out to determine the cause of death.

Listening Test 4

TIME ALLOWED: APPROXIMATELY 30 MINUTES, PLUS 10 MINUTES TO TRANSFER ANSWERS

NUMBER OF QUESTIONS: 40

This test has been written to simulate the IELTS test in its style, format, level of difficulty, question types and length. You should do this test under IELTS test conditions. This means playing the recording only once without pausing or stopping.

Instructions

You will hear four different recordings and you will have to answer questions on what you hear.

There will be time for you to read the instructions and questions before the recording is played. You will also have the opportunity to check your answers.

The recording will be played **ONCE** only.

The test is in four sections. Write your answers on the question sheet as you listen. At the end of Section 4 you have 10 minutes to transfer your answers onto the answer sheet, which is on page 31. When you finish, check the answer key at the back of the book.

Now turn to Section 1 on the next page.

SECTION 1

Questions 1–10

Questions 1–6

Label the floor plan below.

*Choose **FIVE** answers from the floor plan and write the correct letters, **A–I**, next to questions 1–6.*

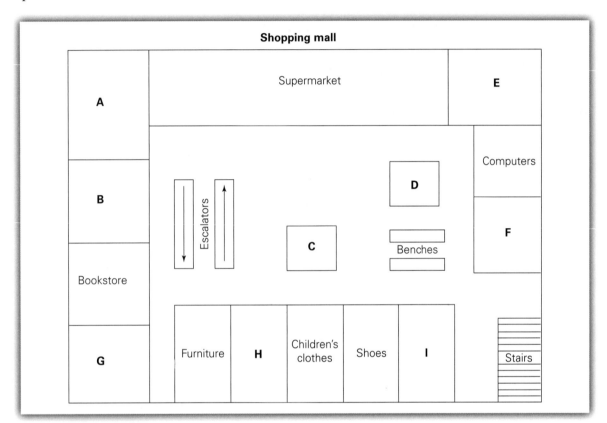

Shopping mall

Supermarket

A

E

Computers

D

B

Escalators

C

F

Benches

Bookstore

G

Furniture

H

Children's clothes

Shoes

I

Stairs

Example

information desk   C

1   children's play centre   ....

2   hairdresser   ....

3   toy store   ....

4   toilets   ....

5   phone kiosk   ....

6   elevator   ....

Questions 7–10

Answer the questions below.

Write **NO MORE THAN TWO WORDS AND/OR A NUMBER** *for each answer.*

7   How much does it cost to leave your car in the car park for four hours? ....

8   What is the minimum age for children at the children's play centre? ....

9   Which level is the food court located on? ....

10   What is located on the top floor of the building? ....

SECTION 2

Questions 11–20

Complete the notes below.

*Write **NO MORE THAN TWO WORDS AND/OR A NUMBER** for each answer.*

The agency

▼ Contented Homes agency began in **11** ………………...……………. .

▼ Agency does most work using the **12** ………………...……………. .

How the system operates

▼ Minimum time period for housesitting is **13** ………………...……………. .

▼ Housesitters do not pay **14** ………………...……………. .

▼ Homeowners check **15** ………………...…………….. of housesitters.

▼ Housesitters have fewer **16** ………………...……………. than normal tenants.

Advantages of having housesitters

▼ Prevent **17** ………………...……………. .

▼ Keep your home clean.

▼ Take care of your **18** ………………...……………. and ………………...……………. .

Charges

▼ Agency charges housesitters **19** ………………...……………. to register.

▼ Agency recommends that homeowners organise **20** ………………...……………. .

Where did a majority of the nationalities listed below settle?

*Choose your answer from the box and write the correct letters, **A–C**, next to questions 21–25.*

You may use any answer more than once.

A Melbourne
B Sydney
C Other places in Australia

---

21 British   ....

22 Chinese   ....

23 Lebanese   ....

24 Malaysians   ....

25 New Zealanders   ....

Questions 26–30

Choose the correct letter, A, B or C.

26 Most migrants chose where to live based on

    A   employment.

    B   community.

    C   real estate.

27 There is a trend for people born in Australia to leave Sydney

    A   because it's becoming too busy and crowded.

    B   due to the inadequate infrastructure.

    C   so they can have more money in retirement.

28 Among people who recently migrated to Australia, the percentage who settled in Sydney and Melbourne was

    A   40%.

    B   50%.

    C   60%.

29 The government is considering encouraging migrants to settle in other areas by

    A   offering tax incentives to employers.

    B   making it easier for farmers to immigrate.

    C   employing people outside Sydney and Melbourne.

30 The number of migrants living in Sydney is likely to be

    A   higher than the statistics indicate.

    B   lower than the statistics indicate.

    C   the same as the statistics indicate.

Questions 31–37

CD 2 • Track 10 *Complete the table below.*

Write **NO MORE THAN THREE WORDS AND/OR A NUMBER** *for each answer.*

Product	Traditional source	Advantages of using hemp
Paper	wood	▼ ready to harvest in **31** .... ▼ no need for **32** ....
Clothing	cotton	▼ needs less **33** .... , fertiliser and pesticides ▼ provides better protection for people against **34** ....
Lamps	**35**	▼ causes less smell
Cars	metal	▼ is **36** .... ▼ decomposes sooner
Fuel	petrol	▼ causes less **37** ....

Questions 38–40

Complete the summary below.

*Choose your answers from the box and write the correct letters, **A–G**, next to questions 38–40.*

A dry	**E** non-toxic
B cheese	**F** shady
C flour	**G** versatile
D long-lasting	

Hemp can be a source of foods and health products. It can produce **38** ....

containing a higher level of protein. It has many applications in the home. Paint made from

hemp is **39** .... Hemp grows well under **40** .... conditions. It is an

environmentally friendly solution to many problems.

LISTENING ANSWER SHEET

Pencil must be used to complete this sheet.

1			21		
2			22		
3			23		
4			24		
5			25		
6			26		
7			27		
8			28		
9			29		
10			30		
11			31		
12			32		
13			33		
14			34		
15			35		
16			36		
17			37		
18			38		
19			39		
20			40		
				Total	

What is in the reading module?

Format of the test	There are three sections of increasing difficulty: **Section 1:** contains two or three short texts, or several shorter texts. Candidates are required to extract general factual information from the texts. **Section 2:** contains two texts that deal with the workplace, such as company policy, business practice, staff training and job applications. **Section 3:** is the general reading section. It contains an extended prose text of a descriptive or instructive type.
Number of questions	40 questions, 1 mark per question Each section contains 12 to 14 questions.
Time allowed	60 minutes
Reading strategies and skills	See detailed guidelines in 'Reading strategies and skills', *Focusing on IELTS: Reading and Writing Skills* (Lindeck, Greenwood and O'Sullivan 2011), pages 29–84.

Question types

The following question types are used in the reading module:

▼ *Multiple choice* – you have to choose one correct answer to a question from four options, or two or three correct options from a set of five or seven.

▼ *Identifying information* – you have to decide whether a statement is true or false according to the information in the passage, or whether no information about the statement is given.

▼ *Identifying writer's views or claims* – you choose 'yes' if a statement agrees with the opinions or claims of the writer, 'no' if the statement contradicts the writer's opinion or argument, or 'not given' if the passage gives no information on what the writer thinks about the statement.

▼ *Matching information* – you have to match the information stated in each question with the relevant paragraph or section in the passage where the information can be found.

▼ *Matching headings* – you have to select the correct heading from the box to match the main idea of each paragraph or section in the passage.

▼ *Matching features* – from a set of possible options, you have to select the correct option that matches the features or characteristics described in each question.

▼ *Matching sentence endings* – you have to choose the correct option from a list in a box to complete a sentence that reflects information given in the passage.

▼ *Sentence completion* – you have to find a word or phrase in the passage that correctly completes a sentence. You may have to write one, two or three words and/or a number.

▼ *Summary/notes/flow-chart/table completion* – you have to either find words or phrases from the text or select words from a box of possible answers to complete a summary or notes of part of the passage, or a table or flow-chart that represents information in the passage. You may have to write one, two or three words and/or a number.

▼ *Diagram label completion* – you have to find words or phrases from the passage to label the parts of a diagram that reflects information in the passage. You may have to write one, two or three words and/or a number.

▼ *Short-answer questions* – you have to write one, two or three words and/or a number to answer brief questions about information in the passage.

In some question types (for example, *identifying information*) the questions follow the same order in which the information occurs in the passage; in other question types (for example, *matching information*), the answers might be located anywhere in the text or texts.

For detailed explanation, see *Focusing on IELTS: Reading and Writing Skills* (Lindeck, Greenwood and O'Sullivan 2011) pages 5–28.

Tips for doing the Reading Test

Make sure you are familiar with each question type so you know what you have to do.

▼ Remember to keep an eye on the time and make sure you have enough time to do all three sections.

▼ If you cannot answer a question after about a minute, move on to the next question and come back later if you have time.

▼ If you cannot answer a question at all, it is better to guess than to leave a blank.

▼ Leave a few minutes at the end of the test to review your answers.

▼ Check for spelling and grammar in items such as short-answer questions.

▼ Check that your response matches the word restrictions given in the instructions (one, two or three words and/or a number).

▼ Take care to write your answers in the correct box on the answer sheet; a correct answer in the wrong box will be marked as incorrect.

▼ Read quickly through each text or set of texts before you look at the questions to get a general idea of the type of information they contain.

▼ In each question, underline the key word that indicates the information you are looking for.

▼ Remember to use the reading skills of skimming for general ideas and scanning for specific information.

▼ Recognise which questions need you to read carefully for concepts (for example, *matching information*) and which require scanning for details (for example, *table completion*).

▼ Remember to look for synonyms and paraphrases of words and ideas in the questions as well as the exact words.

Reading Test 1

ALL ANSWERS MUST BE WRITTEN ON THE ANSWER SHEET.

The test is divided as follows:

Section 1   Questions 1 to 14

Section 2   Questions 15 to 28

Section 3   Questions 29 to 40

Start at the beginning of the test and work through it. You should answer all the questions. If you cannot do a particular question leave it and go on to the next one. You can return to it later.

TIME ALLOWED: 60 MINUTES

NUMBER OF QUESTIONS: 40

Read the advertisements below and answer questions 1–4.

A

TEACHERS NEEDED

Musical Theatre School seeks Drama, Music & Singing teachers

Teachers must have a teaching qualification in at least one of these subject areas plus five years' experience in an appropriate field. Salary negotiable.

Tel. 0444 000 333
Info@nostagefright.com
www.nostagefright.com

B

FILM-MAKING
Summer School

Southern Uni, 6 Jan to 28 Jan
All aspects of practical film-making taught by leading film-makers. Four of our graduates have already won local and international awards for their short films. Students will be charged $150 for the use of professional equipment provided by the Summer School.
Tel. 9876 5432
www.summerschool.blogspot.com

C

Amateur Photography

Avondale Valley TAFE College
3, 4, 7, 8, 9 June
Participants will need to bring their own cameras and will be shown how to pay for their hobby by taking professional photographs. They will also be given assistance in marketing and selling their pictures to a wide range of publications and publicity organisations.
Tel. 9331 1347
www.avv.edu

D

Opera at The Arts Hall
Aida – Verdi

14, 17, 21, 25, 28 Nov
The performance on the 25th will be especially for younger schoolchildren and will include an explanation by an operetta conductor. School parties must be accompanied by teachers or responsible adults.
www.opera-artshall.org
Bookings: 1300 133 331
Evenings 7.30

E

City of Windyhill presents

Free Organic Lunch
With the Air Force Band
Tunes, marches, toccatas and fanfares from Faure, Elgar and JS Bach
During the interval the City of Windyhill Air Cadets will give a display of their marching and drilling skills accompanied by the drums and trumpets of a section of the Air Force Band.
1 pm (60 mins) doors open 12.30 pm
Monday 16 November – Town Hall

F

Modern Theatre Company

When the Bells Start Ringing
Young and old will enjoy this comedy based on the antics of the vicar of a small country village parish when he tries to organise bell ringers for his church.
By Andrea Bonetti
Summer Theatre until 22 Nov.
Booking: 8888 0808
Note: advanced booking is essential as the theatre has limited seating capacity.

G

POTTERY CLASSES

Pottery classes will be held at the Maynard Creative Institute for those interested in adding individual decoration to their homes. The cost of $50 for the course will include tea and biscuits during the break and full use of the kilns. Potting clay will be provided.
17–23 August
Tel. 4526 9981

H

The Swing Revue

Wed 25 November
One night only
A musical journey through the history of jazz
Music from jazz and swing greats: the Dorsey brothers, Benny Goodman, Artie Shaw, Glenn Miller, Billy May, Acker Bilk, Chris Barber and many others. Step out with your partner at the Happy Valley Ballroom and show off your moves, from the Jitterbug to the Jive.
Bookings: http://swing_revue.com

Questions 1–4

Look at the eight advertisements, A–H.

For which advertisements are the following statements true?

Write the correct letter, A–H, in boxes 1–4 on your answer sheet.

NB You may use any letter more than once.

1 A meal is offered at no cost.

2 People will have the opportunity to dance.

3 It is aimed at those interested in cinema.

4 A stage play will be performed.

Look at the diagram below and answer questions 5–10.

How to use phone banking

Press the numbers then press #

Press 1 Account information	Press 2 Bill payments	Press 3 Other services
Then press:	Then press:	Then press:

1 for account balances	**1** to make a payment	**1** to order a statement

2 for a transaction summary	**2** to add to billing list	**2** to request a cheque book

	3 to delete from billing list	**3** to change your PIN

		4 to change your account

		5 to speak to a customer service officer

Questions 5–10

Which combination of numbers would you need to press to receive a particular service?

Write your answers in boxes 5–10 on your answer sheet.

Example	**Answer**
You want to request a cheque book.	3, 2

5   You want to alter your personal identification number.
6   You want to find out how much is in your bank account.
7   You want to deposit some money in someone's account.
8   You want to stop a regular withdrawal.
9   You need to check a printed list of your recent payments.
10   You want to ask about bank loans.

Read the text below and answer questions 11–14.

REDUCE YOUR RISK IN BUSHFIRE AREAS
What you wear is important

Those who live or work in bushfire-prone areas need to take special care during the bushfire season, which is summer. Apart from obvious precautions such as not lighting campfires, not smoking outside and protecting homes or places of work, people should carefully check their clothing to ensure it can also provide suitable protection in the case of a bushfire.

Radiant heat can kill. To protect yourself from radiant heat you need:

▼ long-sleeved overalls or a long-sleeved wool or cotton shirt and long pants made from natural fibres, such as jeans

▼ a wide-brimmed hat

▼ goggles or glasses to protect your eyes

▼ a face mask or moistened towel tied around nose and mouth

▼ sturdy gloves made from natural fibres (not rubber or synthetic)

▼ sturdy shoes or boots with enclosed toes, preferably leather with thick leather soles.

Questions 11–14

Complete the summary below.

*Choose **NO MORE THAN ONE WORD** from the passage for each answer.*

Awareness of bushfires is especially important in **11** ……………..……………. . Clearly, people

should not smoke outside or make **12** ……………..……………. and they need to know what

kind of clothes will protect them in case of a bushfire. To guard against radiant heat, you can

wear long pants with, above the waist, a long-sleeved shirt or **13** ……………..……………. . It is

advisable to protect the eyes, nose and mouth, while the feet can be protected with footwear made

of **14** ……………..……………. .

Read the job advertisement below and answer questions 15–21.

Project Officer

12 months full-time contract (possibility of extension, subject to funding)
(Part-time will be considered.)

$59,700 – $65,100 plus superannuation

WellFare provides excellent community-based services to the elderly and infirm, young disabled people and others with complex support needs in the northern suburbs. WellFare is based in Aldheim in the City of Fraser.

Primary tasks:
- ▼ maintain client information and welfare administration (including all associated paperwork and budget)
- ▼ attend weekly internal meetings and represent WellFare at external meetings as required
- ▼ advise and assist carers
- ▼ supervise carer-focused practices
- ▼ help our elderly and disabled clients integrate into society.

Research and contribution to policy will also form part of the role – the successful applicant will be required to assist with reviewing and developing further initiatives as part of WellFare's strategic plan.

To be considered for this position you will need to have:
- ▼ a degree in a relevant discipline
- ▼ demonstrated experience working in a caring profession
- ▼ experience in record-keeping to meet legislative requirements
- ▼ a Class C driver's licence.

Personal requirements:
- ▼ a supportive and caring nature
- ▼ a willingness to accept responsibility
- ▼ good communication skills
- ▼ the ability to work as part of a team.

Conditions include four weeks' annual holiday, with arrangements to be made in conjunction with colleagues and with the approval of the Project Manager.

A requirement of this position is a satisfactory police records check.

Applications close Wednesday, 23 July.

For more information please call Celine Reeves on 8856 5126.

Do the following statements agree with the information given in the text?

In boxes 15–21 on your answer sheet write

TRUE   if the statement agrees with the information

FALSE   if the statement contradicts the information

NOT GIVEN   if there is no information on this

15   The position will definitely finish in one year.

16   The successful applicant may have to work with aged people.

17   The successful applicant will help decide the organisation's plan for the future.

18   The job particularly involves helping people who have impaired vision.

19   People who have never studied will be considered for this position.

20   Payment will include two weeks' sick leave.

21   The employers want to know if the applicant has broken the law.

Read the text below and answer questions 22–28.

ATHLONE MACHINE PARTS
Company policy on smoking

A In view of recent attention given to the hazards of smoking, the Company is increasingly aware of the need for a new policy on smoking in the workplace, for the health of both smokers and non-smokers among employees. The new policy incorporates both government regulations and the detailed recommendations recently made by the Bridgenorth Health Institute, following its long-term survey on the effects of smoking on health.

B Athlone Machine Parts has decided to implement the new policy on smoking as a matter of urgency. Therefore, from 1 January next year, when on Company property, all employees are required to respect the Company's policy with regard to smoking as set out below.

C While Athlone Machine Parts accepts the rights of employees to smoke during their work breaks, there are certain restrictions in order to comply with government regulations on health and safety. Office workers who smoke are provided with a balcony on Level 2 on which they are permitted to smoke during tea and lunch breaks. Apart from that balcony, employees may smoke on Company premises outdoors at any time, provided that they are a minimum of 10 metres away from any doorway or entrance to a building.

D Smokers are required to dispose of all cigarette butts, matches and packaging both on and surrounding Company premises. Extra bins have been provided especially for this purpose and using them will make the working environment more pleasant for everyone.

E Smoking in offices is forbidden at all times. Non-smokers can use the main lounge for their breaks. Five areas on the factory floor are reserved for non-smokers during their breaks, and smoking in these areas is not permitted at any time. When working on the various machines on the factory floor, smoking is not permitted under any circumstances.

F Failure to comply with any aspect of this policy may result in dismissal from the Company. If you have any queries about this policy, please address them to Julio Santos, HR, or your team leader.

Questions 22–28

The text has six paragraphs, **A–F**.

Which paragraph contains the following information?

*Write the correct letter, **A–F**, in boxes 22–28 on your answer sheet.*

NB You may use any letter more than once.

22 Consequences of disobeying the new rules

23 Locations at which smoking will still be allowed

24 The date when the new rules will come into effect

25 Areas where smoking is banned

26 Reasons behind the new rules

27 What employees should do if they are not sure about the rules

28 How to keep the company premises tidy

Questions 29–34

The text on pages 47–48 has six paragraphs, **A–F**.

Choose the correct heading for each paragraph from the list of headings below.

*Write the correct number, **i–ix**, in boxes 29–34 on your answer sheet.*

List of headings

i	Financial benefits of the plan
ii	Implications of rising sea levels for tourism
iii	How the plan will work
iv	Opposition to the cost of the plan
v	The Dutch take the lead
vi	Historical reasons to guard against disaster
vii	Financial support from other countries for the Dutch plan
viii	Measures taken in the past to safeguard the country
ix	Why the Dutch accepted the plan

---

29 Paragraph A

30 Paragraph B

31 Paragraph C

32 Paragraph D

33 Paragraph E

34 Paragraph F

Read the text below and answer questions 35–40.

A Dutch perspective on climate change

A While most nations view the widely predicted climate change with serious concern, there is a very different view in the Netherlands. With something like one-third of its land surface below sea level, the country has been faced with the threat of major floods for most of its existence. In consequence, Dutch authorities have long been very careful about protecting their land from the ravages of the sea; they last faced serious disruption in the great flood of 1953, when almost 2,000 people died.

B Over the centuries they have planned to augment the available land, protecting the low-lying areas by building bigger and better dykes to keep the sea out. During the last century, they enclosed a huge bay and turned it into the vast inland Lake IJssel, and even drained a large proportion of it, thus increasing the area of dry land for agricultural purposes. The Dutch have always had a close relationship with water. Over the centuries, their fleets enabled them to create a vast empire, which brought them influence and power over far larger nations in addition to considerable prosperity. In their efforts to retain the land they reclaimed from the sea, the Dutch built a vast network of dykes, drainage canals and pumping stations to keep the water at bay in these low-lying areas. The pumps were powered by thousands of windmills. At Kinderdijk, in the south-west, there are still 19 such windmills dating from the 1700s. Although they are no longer used for drainage purposes, they still attract tourists in summer. Yet water has often brought tragedy to the Netherlands, mainly through the bursting of dykes, which have caused many hundreds of deaths, even in the 20th century.

C Now that the world is beginning to agree that increasing world temperatures may cause a global rise in sea level, the Dutch have not waited for scientists and politicians to argue and debate about whether the climatic figures can be trusted and, if so, what to do about them without disrupting jobs and national economies. The Dutch Government has, with the agreement of its population, projected a grand plan, complete with full costing and considerable detail for the next 90 years, which will act as a national defence against the effects of any damage caused by rising sea levels.

D To have the scientific experts, politicians and public all concurring about such a plan within two years is an incredible achievement, but the Dutch have taken this a step further and have already begun to put the plan into action. The Dutch see that such a plan is vital for their own protection, and that the rest of the world cannot be relied upon to agree on a policy in time to give seriously threatened nations such as themselves a chance to take effective countermeasures. The Dutch have therefore attacked the problem of climate change and produced this long-term project, easing local economic and political concerns to such a degree that many see the whole issue as more of a potential bonus than a threat to their existence.

E The project is unusual in many respects. It is not cheap; it will cost about 1.6 billion euros per year for about 40 years, and up to 1.5 billion euros per year for the remaining 50 years. There are no plans to build all dykes higher and stronger, as might be expected; indeed, many of the dykes will be taken down

continued ▶

and in other areas water will be allowed in to reduce the rate of salinity. Sand dug out from the North Sea will be added in vast quantities to many coastal areas to attempt to bring them back to a more natural tidal system. Along the North Sea coast, beach expansion will extend the land seawards by up to a kilometre, which will create further nature reserves. There will be land areas along some major rivers that are to be banned to all development in order to allow the rivers to function more naturally. Funding for the whole project has also been discussed, and it has been agreed in principle that revenues from natural gas reserves from the North Sea will play some part in the project as will part of the Netherlands' very generous civil service pension fund, which is one of the world's largest.

F There appear to be at least three main commercial spin-offs to the project. First, once the system has been proved to be effective, then other nations that are in a similar situation may well seek to benefit from the Dutch experience and be prepared to pay for assistance in solving their own problems. Second, as the project entails the building of dozens of huge stormwater storage tanks, doubling as play areas or car parks in dry weather, the expertise involved could be exported. Third, the creation and selling of enormous quantities of fresh water to countries that need it may be, in the long run, the most valuable export earner. Part of Lake IJssel is to be converted into a freshwater storage area. The Dutch themselves have no shortage of fresh water because the annual rainfall is normally quite sufficient for their domestic purposes.

Questions 35–40

*Choose the correct letter, **A**, **B**, **C** or **D**.*

Write the correct letter in boxes 35–40 on your answer sheet.

35   Why have the Dutch always made great efforts to save their land from flooding?

    A   There was a serious flood in 1953.

    B   The nation has a heavy average rainfall.

    C   A large portion of their country is below sea level.

    D   A lake is in danger of overflowing.

36   Why have the Dutch kept 300-year-old windmills?

    A   They are used to store fresh water.

    B   They appeal to holidaymakers.

    C   The windmills pump water and generate electricity from wind.

    D   They are still used to drain water from areas below sea level.

37 The Dutch Government has acted on climate change because they

    A   have access to more advanced scientific data.

    B   are particulary concerned about employment.

    C   have responded to public pressure.

    D   are unwilling to delay while different groups reach agreement.

38 To limit flooding in the country, which procedure might appear unusual?

    A   The removal of some sea walls.

    B   The use of sand from the North Sea.

    C   The reclamation of land from the sea.

    D   The prevention of land development along river banks.

39 Where does the Dutch Government plan to increase the amount of land?

    A   Along the banks of the major rivers.

    B   On the North Sea coast.

    C   In existing nature reserves.

    D   On most of the main dykes.

40 Which source is expected to help finance the plan?

    A   Freshwater sales.

    B   Pension funds.

    C   Sales of agricultural produce.

    D   Profits from water storage.

Reading Test 2

ALL ANSWERS MUST BE WRITTEN ON THE ANSWER SHEET.

The test is divided as follows:

Section 1   Questions 1 to 14

Section 2   Questions 15 to 28

Section 3   Questions 29 to 40

Start at the beginning of the test and work through it. You should answer all the questions. If you cannot do a particular question leave it and go on to the next one. You can return to it later.

TIME ALLOWED: 60 MINUTES

NUMBER OF QUESTIONS: 40

Read the advertisements below and answer questions 1–5.

Fairbairn Tutoring Summer School

Fairbairn Tutoring is offering a three-week course to help prepare students for the new school year. Each of the six courses is for three days per week and is taught by fully qualified and registered teachers.

A

Beginners French

This course is for those who expect to start a French course at Year 7 level. It teaches basic French pronunciation as well as the first elements of grammar.

Teacher: Mme de Fraîches

Days: Tue/Wed/Thu

Times: 9–12, 1–5 pm

Cost: $1,500

B

Senior Physics

The Senior Physics course will suit those students who have reached Year 10 level and wish to study Physics at senior level in Years 11 and 12.

Teacher: Dr M Phillips

Days: Mon/Wed/Thu

Times: 9–12, 1–5 pm

Cost: $2,000

C

English Language

Students in Years 9 or 10 will find this English course helpful. It is designed to improve the basic knowledge of grammar and to extend their vocabulary as native English speakers.

Teacher: Mrs E Williams

Days: Mon/Thu/Fri

Times: 9–12, 1–5 pm

Cost: $1,600

D

Geography

This course will assist students who wish to concentrate on Geography when they enter senior level this year.

Teacher: Mr M McCormick

Days: Mon/Tue/Fri

Times: 9–12, 1–5 pm

Cost: $1,800

E

Mathematics

This course is a remedial course for those students in Years 8–10 who have had difficulties in understanding mathematical concepts.

Teacher: Dr Ruth Morrissey

Days: Tue/Wed/Fri

Times: 9–12, 1–5 pm

Cost: $1,700

F

English – ESL

This course is designed for younger students (Years 7 and 8) whose native language is not English. They are shown how to improve their confidence in the skills of reading, writing, speaking and listening.

Teacher: Mr J Harrison

Days: Mon/Wed/Fri

Times: 9–12, 1–5 pm

Cost: $1,600

Questions 1–5

Look at the six advertisements, A–F.

For which advertisements are the following statements true?

Write the correct letter, A–F, in boxes 1–5 on your answer sheet.

NB You may use any letter more than once.

1   This course is for students who speak a language other than English as their first language.

2   This course would be useful for a student who is weak in areas such as arithmetic or geometry.

3   Students who intend to learn a language other than English could do this course.

4   This course will suit a person hoping to concentrate on science.

5   None of the classes in this course are on consecutive days.

Read the advertisement below and answer questions 6–8.

Berivale Community Centre Walks

Our Centre organises a number of walks once a month in picturesque Trentham. For details of dates and times call the Berivale Community Centre on 8005 8111.

▼ Walks are usually held between 8.30 am and 2.30 pm and are led by an experienced guide along established tracks.

▼ Our next scheduled walk is on 10 June. The first 3 km take the walkers through the old parts of Trentham. In the next 5 km, walkers will experience the old-growth forest and the occasional glimpse of a sleeping koala. The final 2 km bring the party back to the railway station via the town library. The walk is 10 km in total.

▼ Cost is $8.00 plus train ticket to be purchased prior to meeting. Train tickets are from $3.00 to $5.00 – there are fare discounts for seniors and students.

▼ Please meet at Berivale Station near platforms 5 and 6 from 9 am. Participants are reminded that the train to Trentham departs at 9.20 am and the return train to Berivale at 2.40 pm.

Questions 6–8

Complete the summary below.

Choose **NO MORE THAN ONE NUMBER** *from the text for each answer.*

Write your answers in boxes 6–8 on your answer sheet.

The Trentham track

On 10 June, participants will walk for **6** ……………..…….....……. kilometres altogether, taking in

the sights of the Trentham region. They must pay **7** …………..……….....…….. dollars in addition to

the railway ticket. Those who wish to join in are asked to start meeting at **8** ………..…..……... am.

Read the text below and answer questions 9–14.

Meriton Library Services

The Meriton Library is a branch of the larger Oldfield Library Services organisation and Meriton borrowers have access to all books kept in the organisation's seven branch libraries. These include the very large Oldfield College library, which contains over 750,000 books.

Membership

▼ Anyone can join the library – it's free. You can join at any Meriton branch or online at http://catalogue.meriton.shire.org.

▼ Proof of name and current address is required for membership.

▼ If you join online, you need to bring current identification and proof of address on your first visit to the library. If you're under 18 you will need to have the application form signed by a parent or guardian.

Membership also entitles borrowers to use library facilities such as computers, scanners and Internet access.

Borrowing

▼ You must present your library card to borrow or use a computer.

▼ You can borrow up to 25 items at a time.

▼ Books, talking books: 3-week loans.

▼ Magazines, DVDs and videos: 2-week loans.

▼ Reserved items may have a shorter loan period.

▼ Fines will apply for late return of all library items.

Renewals

▼ Renewals can be done by phone on 8300 1900, on the website at http://catalogue.meriton.shire.org or in person at the library.

▼ Items reserved by another member cannot be renewed.

Requests

▼ Books can be requested from other branches or from other library services via the interlibrary loan system.

▼ Interlibrary loan requests are free but are limited to three items at any one time.

Questions 9–14

Do the following statements agree with the information given in the text?

In boxes 9–14 on your answer sheet write

TRUE   if the statement agrees with the information

FALSE   if the statement contradicts the information

NOT GIVEN   if there is no information on this

9   Payment is required to make use of the listed library services.

10   A password is needed to join on the Internet.

11   Children under 18 wanting to join need permission from a responsible adult.

12   Borrowing more than a dozen items at a time is forbidden.

13   If somebody wants to borrow a book that you have, you may not extend the loan.

14   If you order a book from another library, you need to allow three days for its arrival.

SECTION 2

Questions 15–21

The text on page 56 has seven paragraphs, **A–G**.

Choose the correct heading for each paragraph from the list of headings below.

*Write the correct number, **i–x**, in boxes 15–21 on your answer sheet.*

List of headings

i	Remuneration and working conditions
ii	Experience and qualifications
iii	Contact details
iv	Reason for new position
v	Supervisor meeting
vi	Possible future promotion
vii	Recommendations from colleagues
viii	Qualities of a successful candidate
ix	Selection procedure
x	Retirement bonus

---

15 Paragraph A

16 Paragraph B

17 Paragraph C

18 Paragraph D

19 Paragraph E

20 Paragraph F

21 Paragraph G

Read the text below and answer questions 15–21.

INTERNAL AUDITOR REQUIRED

A Frankstown Books has expanded its business over the last two years and is seeking to appoint an auditor from among its present employees to oversee accounts. The position is an internal one and is offered to staff who fulfil the conditions detailed below.

B The successful applicant must have been with Frankstown Books for at least two years and will have a tertiary accounting or business degree of Bachelor level or higher. Membership of a professional organisation would be seen as an advantage, particularly if the applicant takes an active role in the organisation.

C Applicants for this position should first discuss their application with their Line Manager and supply a letter of referral from this manager as well as written recommendations from staff in two other departments. Letters of referral and/or references from previous employers will also be taken into account in assessing the applicant's suitability for the position.

D Applicants must be prepared to be called for an interview between 23 and 26 February, and a final decision will be announced on Tuesday 2 March. Unsuccessful applicants will also be notified by internal memo, but their details will be noted in the case of further positions becoming available at a later date.

E The successful applicant will take up duties on Monday 15 March and will be directly responsible to the General Manager. It is expected that the position will be upgraded to a senior position with a staff of two assistants within two years. If the position is to be upgraded, the incumbent will be given three months' notice in order to make enquiries regarding the assistant positions.

F The position carries an allowance of $17,120 in addition to the salary already paid. All other conditions such as superannuation, sick leave and holiday pay will remain the same. The salary will be reviewed annually, and, in the case of the position being upgraded, will be substantially increased.

G Any staff member wishing to be considered for this position should contact Sally Jones on Extension 78 in the Human Relations Office by 5 pm on Friday 19 February. Regrettably, late applications will not be considered except under very exceptional circumstances; such late applications must be accompanied by a detailed letter of explanation.

Read the text below and answer questions 22–28.

MEMO TO ALL STAFF
Employee use of company computers

In the past, company management has been very reluctant to interfere in the content of company computers used by employees, and has accepted that occasional private downloading has occurred without taking serious action. However, there have recently been more serious problems causing a negative effect on many of the company's computers and, consequently, staff are asked to study this memo and to follow its guidelines diligently.

Virus protection

There have been difficulties reported to management over the last two weeks regarding viruses in the computer system. These viruses have apparently entered via private emails sent to staff. While management spends a considerable sum of money in trying to protect the computer network, it is impossible to prevent *all* viruses from getting in without spending a much greater proportion of the company's profits on virus protection. Management is reluctant to do this as it would reduce the number of staff that can be employed.

Restricted use

While management does not wish to impose unnecessary restrictions on employees using the company's computers, staff are required to limit their private use of emails and Net surfing to formal work breaks only, and to check that all incoming emails do not carry a virus. Conducting private business during working hours constitutes a breach of contract between an employee and the company which could lead to an employee's discharge from the company.

Legal issues

An employee of another local business has recently been dismissed for downloading illegal material onto a company computer. This has not happened in this company but staff are reminded that management has the right to check the contents of any company computer at any time, and that illegal material on a staff member's computer will be reported to the police for possible criminal charges. All employees are asked to check the contents of any company computer they use and to report any content that they feel has no right to be there. They should also record the date and time they find such content in order that management can check when any illegal material has been downloaded.

Questions 22–28

Complete the summary below.

*Choose **NO MORE THAN THREE WORDS** from the text for each answer.*

Write your answers in boxes 22–28 on your answer sheet.

Computer use

Until recently, the employers have not wished to dictate how workers use company computers but now, as issues have arisen, they are concerned about **22** ……………..…………… that have recently appeared. Management fears that the expense involved in solving this problem could result in cutbacks to **23** ……………..…………… .

Workers may only use company computers for private purposes in **24** ……………..…………… . Failure to follow these rules is a **25** ……………..…………… .

A **26** ……………..…………… in the area has already fired a worker for misusing a work computer. Workers found to have **27** ……………..…………… on their computers may face dismissal. **28** ……………..…………… are a potential consequence of staff breaking the law.

Read the text below and answer questions 29–40.

THE FEZZAN

In the south-west of Libya, a region called Fezzan is an inaccessible place full of sand seas, dry river beds, mountains, plateaus and savanna. Between 500 BC and 500 AD an estimated 100,000 people farmed and thrived here, in an area that receives less than an inch of rain a year and many years none at all. This is a waterless sea of sand and stone, where scorpions infest, poisonous snakes slither and the sun has no mercy. Libya is big – a slab the size of Italy, France, Spain and Germany combined – and almost all of its six million people live huddled on the Mediterranean coast. 95% of Libya is desert, 20% is sand dunes, and not a single river runs through it. The Libyan Sahara holds the world's heat record (136°F) and can chill the bones on a winter night.

Yet it has not always been like this. There are, improbably, many tiny gem-coloured lakes – some purple, some orange from minerals and algae – that are dried-up remainders of a previous time when groundwater lay closer to the surface than it does today. It's hard to imagine, but a lake the size of England, Lake Megafezzan, gleamed here about 200,000 years ago, when rainfall was abundant, and ancient channels testify that rivers ran to the centre of the desert.

Climate change has been like an on-off switch in the Sahara. In dry times the lakes dwindled and the plants declined to niches. Then, when moister times returned, the lakes filled and parts of the Sahara were transformed to savanna. Human communities have pulsed here like the explosion of plants after a rare rain. When moist eras visited, they thrived. When the dry times returned they shrank or collapsed.

Waterways of long ago can be located from space. Using radar images taken from satellites, scientists have been able to map the location of mineral residues from ancient lakes and springs, then steer paleoanthropologists to the spots. Here, stone tools, arrowheads, fireplaces, graves and other clues to human occupation have been discovered.

The earliest modern humans in the region were hunters and gatherers who lived in a savanna landscape about 130,000 years ago. These people cleared out when the rains tapered off about 70,000 years ago, but then the rains returned and people moved in again. This back-and-forth migration is called the Saharan pump, a movement of people in and out of northern Africa as the climate shifted. Scratched on the desert rocks are memories of a wetter Sahara, when water-dependent creatures such as lions, elephants and rhinoceroses lived here.

A curious thing happened when the most recent wet phase ended. About 5,000 years ago the rains stopped once more, the lakes disappeared, and the deserts took hold. Yet this time the people stayed. Rock art suggests they had already made the transition from hunting to raising livestock. Next came the rise of a society that would begin building towns and make the transition to agriculture: the Garamantian civilization.

The Garamantes flourished here in a climate much like that of the Sahara today. Many scholars assumed they were desert nomads, but excavations at their capital city, Garama (near modern-day Jarmah), and land surveys have shown that they were a sedentary people living off savanna agriculture. They constructed a sophisticated irrigation system that allowed them to grow wheat, barley, sorghum, date palms and olives. Underground canals tapped into groundwater and directed it to fields without loss to evaporation. Roughly 600 miles of these canals can still be detected. The system

continued ▶

worked well for hundreds of years. And then the 'fossil' water, stored up in wet times, started to give out and the civilization collapsed.

The Sahara seems like a barrier at first glance, severing Africa into two pieces. But for the humans who have lived in Libya for thousands of years, it has been a corridor. Gold and ivory and slaves came north from sub-Saharan Africa; olive oil, wine, glass and other goods from the Mediterranean flowed south. This creates a lasting image in our minds; the caravan wending its way through huge sand dunes. The Saharan corridor may even have been one of the pathways our ancestors followed when they left the eastern part of the continent to populate the rest of the world. Scholars have long assumed that early humans expanded beyond sub-Saharan Africa into Eurasia by migrating either along the Nile River and across the Sinai or across the Red Sea.

Questions 29–33

Answer the questions below.

*Choose **NO MORE THAN THREE WORDS** from the text for each answer.*

Write your answers in boxes 29–33 on your answer sheet.

29   What causes Libya's dry lakes to be multicoloured?

30   What evidence on the ground led scientists to places where water used to be?

31   What name is given to the frequent changing of population in the north African desert?

32   What evidence indicates that people in the Fezzan had stopped living as hunter-gatherers more than 5,000 years ago?

33   What did earlier people build beneath the ground to avoid losing water into the air?

Questions 34–40

Choose the correct letter A, B, C or D.

Write your answers in boxes 34–40 on your answer sheet.

34 Libya's population is

    A   concentrated in one part of the country.

    B   lower than it was 2,000 years ago.

    C   comparable to that of European countries.

    D   spread evenly throughout the desert.

35 Lake Megafezzan was originally much larger than it is now because

    A   the groundwater was lower.

    B   cooler temperatures prevented water loss.

    C   it rained more in that area in the past.

    D   the mineral content in the area was higher.

36 Human communities in the Sahara have

    A   increased and decreased according to the climate conditions.

    B   steadily shrunk due to the erratic supply of water.

    C   depended on the cultivation of plants.

    D   withstood heavy rain in the past.

37 What happened 5,000 years ago for the first time in the Sahara?

    A   Several waterways dried up.

    B   A time of prosperity finished.

    C   People started drawing on the walls of caves.

    D   Humans remained in the area when the weather became dry.

38 The Garamantian civilisation was based on

    A   migration with flocks of animals.

    B   hunting and gathering plants.

    C   land cultivation.

    D   livestock raising.

39 The reason for the fall of the Garamantes was broadly that

    A   irrigation was unable to cope with the population growth.

    B   there was a sudden change in the climate.

    C   the groundwater supplies ran out.

    D   there was too much evaporation from the oases.

40 In the final paragraph, the writer stresses that the Sahara

    A   has presented challenges to humans for many years.

    B   has had an important role as a passage.

    C   should be the subject of further study.

    D   divides the continent in half.

Reading Test 3

ALL ANSWERS MUST BE WRITTEN ON THE ANSWER SHEET.

The test is divided as follows:

Section 1   Questions 1 to 14

Section 2   Questions 15 to 29

Section 3   Questions 30 to 40

Start at the beginning of the test and work through it. You should answer all the questions. If you cannot do a particular question leave it and go on to the next one. You can return to it later.

TIME ALLOWED: 60 MINUTES

NUMBER OF QUESTIONS: 40

Read the notice below and answer questions 1–4.

Notice to passengers
Alterations to the Denton to Launceford railway timetable

The Launceford railway bridge is under repair and the following arrangements will apply from Denton from 4 June until 30 September this year.

The changes particularly apply to passengers travelling from Denton to Launceford, but other passengers using this route should be aware of alterations to the service.

The additional bus services will be provided by the Launceford Bus Company.

▼ The 8.15 to Launceford will terminate at Bickley and passengers will be taken by bus on to Launceford, arriving at Launceford Station at 9.20 am.

▼ The 9.20 express will not stop at Bickley or Harringby, and passengers for Launceford should not board this train.

▼ The 10.35 to Launceford will travel via Harringby, arriving at Launceford at 11.42 am.

▼ The 1.40 express, normally non-stop, will pause at Bickley to allow passengers to get off and travel on by bus to Launceford. The bus will arrive at Launceford Station at 2.25 pm.

▼ The 3.55 and 5.25 to Launceford will both stop at Bickley and buses will take passengers to Launceford Station, arriving at 5 pm and 6.30 pm respectively.

The Railway Company regrets any inconvenience.

Questions 1–4

Answer the questions below.

*Choose **NO MORE THAN THREE WORDS AND/OR A NUMBER** from the text for each answer.*

Write your answers in boxes 1–4 on your answer sheet.

1   How will passengers on the 8.15 arrive at Launceford Station?

2   When will passengers travelling via Harringby get to Launceford?

3   Where will Launceford passengers on the 1.40 leave the train?

4   At what time will passengers on the 3.55 service arrive in Launceford?

Read the advertisements below and answer questions 5–10.

Forrester Community Centre courses

A

PILATES

Pilates offers gentle exercises designed to build muscle strength and body balance, and to assist the development of relaxation techniques. The exercises are especially useful for adults whose occupation requires long periods of sitting at a desk.

Classes are suitable for both teenagers and adults.

Times:
Tuesdays and Fridays
6.30 pm – 7.30 pm

Casual rate of $10 per session is available ($75 for the term)

B

JEWELLERY MAKING

Learn basic beading and jewellery techniques in a fun, social environment. Express your sense of style and perhaps earn a little extra pocket money by selling your products.

Basic materials and tools provided. Extra pieces available at low cost.

Times:
Tuesdays 6 pm – 7.30 pm

Dates:
6 October – 8 December

Cost: $36 per term

C

SOCIAL DANCE

Dance New Vogue, Latin and Modern to delightful music every Wednesday night.

A revision class to brush up those steps will be held at 7 pm.

When:
every Wednesday
8 pm – 10.30 pm

Cost:
$80 per term or
$10 per session

D

MULTICULTURAL WOMEN'S SEWING PROGRAM

This program supports women who want to learn to sew. The program is supported by volunteers. Skills developed include sewing machine use, hand-sewing, cutting and dressmaking. Learn exotic techniques from other cultures.

Dates: 7, 8 and 9 October

Times: 9.30 am – 1 pm

Cost: $10 per term

E

POTTERY

Be amazed by what you can create! Use either pottery wheels or hand-building techniques to create your own ceramic masterpiece and develop your own style. The content can be adapted according to the individual interests and requirements of each student.

Dates:
7 October – 16 December

When:
Wednesdays 6 pm – 9 pm

Cost:
$110 plus materials

F

CREATIVE CARD MAKING

Birthday, anniversary, celebration, thank-you cards – the opportunities are endless! Create memorable cards for your loved ones.

All materials supplied.

Dates:
8 October – 10 December

When:
Thursdays
1 pm – 2.30 pm

Cost:
$15 per term

Questions 5–10

Look at the six advertisements, A–F.

Which advertisement mentions the following?

Write the correct letter, A–F, in boxes 5–10 on your answer sheet.

NB You may use any letter more than once.

5	needlework and clothes making
6	cost of basic materials not included in price
7	a practice session before the main class
8	suitability for people who work at a computer all day
9	a vigorous activity for those who like to meet other people
10	possible financial profit for participants

Read the notice below and answer questions 11–14.

OFFICE SECURITY

A recent attempt by a staff member to enter company premises last weekend caused a security scare. Although the matter turned out to be quite innocent, staff are reminded of the following security arrangements after the close of business at 5.30 pm on weekdays and over the weekend:

▼ A security officer will lock every office at 6 pm on weekdays.

▼ Any staff member who wishes to may stay for the purpose of completing unfinished business but must inform the security office on ext. 367 and arrange for a security staff officer to check that the office is locked afterwards.

▼ Senior management personnel must also inform the security office if they wish to enter or remain in the building outside normal office hours.

The security office will ensure that the buildings and car park are patrolled at hourly intervals during the night and on weekends.

All staff are asked to be vigilant and to immediately report any suspicious activity to the security office at any time.

Questions 11–14

Answer the questions below.

*Choose **NO MORE THAN THREE WORDS** from the text for each answer.*

Write your answers in boxes 11–14 on your answer sheet.

11 What resulted when a worker tried to get into the office after hours?

12 For what purpose is a staff member permitted to stay in an office outside business hours?

13 How often do security officers check the premises outside normal working hours?

14 What should staff tell security about when the company is open for business?

Questions 15–21

The text on page 68 has seven job advertisements, **A–G**.

Choose the correct advertised title for each position from the list below.

*Write the correct number, **i–xi**, in boxes 15–21 on your answer sheet.*

List of titles

i	Quality controller
ii	Managing director
iii	Research department manager
iv	Office assistant
v	Caretaker
vi	Information technology engineer
vii	Shoemaking apprentice
viii	Human resources manager
ix	Drilling machine operator
x	Production supervisor
xi	Marketing officer

---

15 Position A

16 Position B

17 Position C

18 Position D

19 Position E

20 Position F

21 Position G

Read the text below and answer questions 15–21.

WHITLAND SHOE MANUFACTURING

Whitland Shoe Manufacturing is opening a new factory in the northern suburbs of the city and offers the following new positions:

A This is a senior position requiring a minimum of ten years' experience in footwear studies as well as an ability to report on developments in the trade. A tertiary degree or equivalent in Business Studies is a condition for any applicant for this position. A company car and petrol allowance are available and some rental assistance is also included in the remuneration for this senior position.

B No experience is necessary, as on-the-job training will be given in the use of hand and machine tools, stitching and soling. The applicant must commit to a minimum of three years at the company.

C This person will be in charge of staffing and will report directly to the Chief Executive Officer of the company. Experience or a recognised qualification in Human Resource Management is a required condition for the position. A company car and petrol allowance are provided for this senior position.

D This is a junior position and the successful applicant will have basic typing and shorthand skills as well as knowledge of common clerical practices. This position would suit a younger person applying directly from school or college.

E We are looking for a responsible, hardworking person to maintain the cleanliness of the building. Duties involve sweeping, vacuuming and mopping, as well as replenishing supplies to the kitchenette and restrooms. Must take on pest control duties if the need arises.

F This is a position of responsibility. The successful applicant will supervise the leatherworkers in the factory. Two references concerning the applicant's staff management skills from previous employers should be supplied in supporting the application.

G This is a position for a person with at least ten years' experience in assessing the soundness of products, preferably in the footwear/textiles industry. At least three references from previous employers specifying the experience of the applicant are required for this position.

Note that Whitland Shoe Manufacturing is an equal opportunity employer and all positions are available to applicants of either gender. The Company's Human Resources Office may be able to assist in finding accommodation for successful applicants for all the above positions. Further details can be obtained from Mrs Dalhousie on 2100 2566 887 ext. 21.

Read the text below and answer questions 22–29.

COMPANY TRAINING POLICY

The Company is instituting a new retraining policy for all staff who wish to upgrade their qualifications. Upgraded qualifications recognised by the Company will be taken into consideration with regard to salaries. Potential applicants should study the following notes:

- Any application for training must be for a qualification that benefits the employee and is in the Company's interest. An upgrade of an applicant's current qualification is acceptable.

- All training applications will be considered on their merits by a board of senior managers; however, the board's decision will be final and not open to further negotiation.

- Applicants should contact the Head of Department for advice and a recommendation must be given in writing and signed by the Head of Department. References from colleagues of equal status in the Company are not acceptable.

- The Company will contribute 50% of the cost for external training to a maximum of $2,000. In individual cases there may be exceptions to this rule.

- Leave from company duties may be granted in the case of successful applicants for external training for a maximum of two days per week for a period of three months.

- Internally run courses will incur no cost to the participants. Any materials required will be supplied at Company expense.

- Staff who upgrade their qualifications with financial assistance from their employer will be required, as a condition of acceptance, to guarantee in writing to remain a further period of 12 months with the Company. A staff member who leaves within this time frame will forfeit any holiday pay.

- Under no circumstances will any employee be required to undertake training but the Company hopes that staff will give serious consideration to the offer.

Questions 22–25

Complete the summary using the list of words, A–H, below.

Write the correct letter, A–H, in boxes 22–25 on your answer sheet.

A promotion	**E** community
B time off	**F** equipment
C vacation allowance	**G** wages
D employer	**H** reputation

The company encourages its workers to upgrade their qualifications. If an employee chooses to do further training, this will be a factor affecting their **22** .... An employee can apply for financial assistance with training that will help the applicant and be of value to the **23** .... In addition to funding, employees may be given **24** .... to complete external courses. If an applicant receives money for training and then leaves the company in less than a year, that applicant will forgo any **25** ....

Questions 26–29

Do the following statements agree with the information in the text?

In boxes 26–29 on your answer sheet write

TRUE	if the statement agrees with the information
FALSE	if the statement contradicts the information
NOT GIVEN	if there is no information on this

26   A rejected application may be accepted after discussion with the employee.

27   An applicant's departmental chief must agree to a recommendation for a training course.

28   An applicant will be required to pay the full cost of an external course.

29   A university degree is preferable to a three-month training course.

Read the text below and answer questions 30–40.

Truth about termites

Termites are famous for causing damage to houses, but in fact many of them are harmless to householders and they are, in any case, an important link in the natural environment. Termites are the same size as ants and are often referred to as 'white ants', but they are not actually ants: the ant has a very thin waist whereas a termite does not. They date from about 120 million years ago, well before the first flowering plants. They are, like ants, social insects and live in colonies comprising various castes in nests. As they are soft-bodied insects and prone to drying out, termites are usually hidden away in their nests, underground, or in whatever they are feeding on. Some types can spend time above ground by building external tubes through which they move.

While termites are mostly thought of as destroyers of houses, some species construct amazing houses of their own. The best known of these are probably the termite mounds found in northern Australia, which are always aligned north–south. Some termite mounds can reach an impressive 6 metres tall and several metres across, all built by insects that are only about 5 millimetres long. That would be like humans constructing a building that is 1 kilometre high, over several city blocks, and doing it in the dark. However, not all termites build such massive constructions. One type of very destructive termite nests in roots or trunks of trees, and its nests are linked to underground parts of the colony via tunnels built on the outside of the tree as well as inside the tree itself.

A termite colony normally consists of a queen and king who together are the primary reproductive insects; workers that cannot reproduce, fly or see; soldier termites with the same features; plus eggs and young termites. A small number of young will develop to become queens or kings and will grow wings – these are called alates and will set off on a colonising flight in the warmer months. Sometimes all nests of the same type in an area release their alates at the same time.

Of these young alates, only a few will survive to found a colony. When they succeed, they will shed their wings and the males and females will form pairs. The new king and queen then seek out a place to start a nest, seal themselves into a small chamber, and then after a few days the queen will begin to lay her eggs. She grows into an large, egg-laying machine about 30 millimetres in diameter, capable of laying more than 1,000 eggs per day.

The soldiers defend the colony and are well equipped for this task. There are two distinct types: one has large jaws and the other has the ability to give off a sticky, repellent secretion to drive off invaders. Worker termites are the most numerous caste in the colony and are very busy little creatures. Not only do they gather food, but they also feed the rest of the colony, themselves and the soldiers. They also repair any damage done to the nest, but rarely venture outside as they dry out too easily.

Licensed pest controllers who specialise in termite control are able to identify the main pest species. They can also advise on whether the termites they find are likely to attack a house, shed or fences. For example, some types of insect will damage a tree but not feed on a wooden structure. Another species can travel about 50 metres underground and, if a garden is a source of this type, then preventative action must be taken.

The householder can implement several ways to prevent termite damage before calling in the experts, such as keeping stacks of timber and firewood dry and away from the house.

continued ▶

Removing fallen branches and stumps will also help, as will treating fences, sheds and other garden structures, or perhaps using metal instead of wood for buildings. It is wise to avoid creating garden beds against the walls of houses, and the use of railway sleepers (unless they are specifically treated against termites) to edge garden beds or paths is likewise not recommended. Hoses, taps and gutters sometimes leak and such leaks need to be stopped. Outlets for hot water systems and air conditioners should drain away from the house. There are commercially available bait stations that are an effective monitoring tool for householders to check whether they have an infestation. However, termite treatment is highly regulated. It is illegal to treat termite problems with some insecticides and chemical treatments must be applied by a licensed pest controller.

But despite the damage some species cause to homes, termites are vital in the ecosystem. They play a major role in recycling dead wood, and in the formation and turnover of soil. They are also a useful source of food for birds, lizards, many other small mammals and, in some countries, even people.

Questions 30–34

*Complete each sentence with the correct ending, **A–H**, below.*

Write your answers in boxes 30–34 on your answer sheet.

30 Termite societies contain

31 Certain termite colonies take the form of

32 Termite workers have

33 The termite queens have

34 Termites generally provide

A wooden chambers.

B a source of food for larger creatures.

C several classes of termites.

D neither flying ability nor sight.

E two defence methods.

F a much larger body than the soldiers.

G different types of ant.

H tall, wide nests.

Questions 35–40

Choose the correct letter A, B, C or D.

Write your answers in boxes 35–40 on your answer sheet.

35   Which description best fits termites?

   A   Dark-coloured insects that cause serious damage to buildings.

   B   A type of ant that spends most of the time in the open air.

   C   Similar to ants in size, but with differently shaped bodies.

   D   Flying insects with hard bodies.

36   What are alates?

   A   The only termites who can produce young.

   B   Termites that emerge from eggs.

   C   The young worker-class termites.

   D   The defenders of the colony.

37   What will the queens in a nest do?

   A   Drive the male out after several days.

   B   Produce eggs alone in an enclosed spot.

   C   Stay with the male and produce the young of the colony.

   D   Lay thousands of eggs before she is too large for her mate.

38   What do the worker termites do?

   A   They mate and look after the young.

   B   They defend the colony against attack.

   C   They fly out to find sites for new colonies.

   D   They see to the nutrition and servicing of the colony.

39   Which termite control method should a non-expert householder use?

   A   Cutting down trees and removing them.

   B   Spraying chemicals around the walls of a house.

   C   Taking wet wood away from alongside the home.

   D   Ensuring there are plentiful sources of water to flush out the insects.

40   A suitable title for the text would be

   A   'Harmful Australian insects'.

   B   'Eco-friendly insects of northern Australia'.

   C   'How to protect your house from termites'.

   D   'Types and habits of termites'.

Reading Test 4

ALL ANSWERS MUST BE WRITTEN ON THE ANSWER SHEET.

The test is divided as follows:

Section 1   Questions 1 to 14

Section 2   Questions 15 to 28

Section 3   Questions 29 to 40

Start at the beginning of the test and work through it. You should answer all the questions. If you cannot do a particular question leave it and go on to the next one. You can return to it later.

TIME ALLOWED: 60 MINUTES

NUMBER OF QUESTIONS: 40

Read the evening television guide below and answer questions 1–7.

<table>
<tr><td colspan="3" align="center">Evening TV guide</td></tr>
<tr><td>Channel 1</td><td>Channel 2</td><td>Channel 3</td></tr>
<tr valign="top"><td>

6.00 News
6.30 Sports Roundup
7.00 Today Comment on the day's events
7.30 Our Young Minds University team quiz
8.30 Movie: Firestorm A huge city fire breaks out and the army is called in. PGR
10.00 Late News
10.10 Pet Care Looking after pets
10.30 Late Movie: His Next Girlfriend A man meets a girl with an unusual talent. Horror film. MA
12.00 All Night Show

</td><td>

6.00 Overseas News News from around the world
7.00 World Sport
7.15 Simon Says Humorous comment on the news
7.30 Was Koche Ich? German cooking series. G (German with subtitles)
8.00 Cities of the World James visits some of his favourite places. G
8.30 Documentary: The Latest Building Styles Series illustrating what modern architects are trying. G
9.00 Movie: Les Gosses A group of Paris kids get into trouble. PGR (French with subtitles)

</td><td>

6.00 Sport
6.30 News Summary
6.35 Celebrity News Lives of the rich and famous
6.45 The Top Ten Pop music series
7.00 Get Rich Quick General knowledge quiz with money prizes. G
7.30 Where Are They Now? Series on the lives of old film stars. M
8.00 You Look Good! Series on beauty tips. PGR
8.30 The Fuzz British comic police series. M
9.30 NY Patrol US police series. M

</td></tr>
<tr><td colspan="3">

Program viewer classification:
G – General
PGR – Parental guidance recommended
M – Mature adult
MA – Mature audience, not suited for children under 15

</td></tr>
</table>

Questions 1–7

Answer the questions below.

*Choose **NO MORE THAN THREE WORDS AND/OR A NUMBER** from the text for each answer.*

Write your answers in boxes 1–7 on your answer sheet.

1   Which television channel shows programs in a language other than English?

2   Which channel is showing a film that children under 15 should not watch at all?

3   Which program gives financial rewards to contestants?

4   Which program makes fun of current events?

5   Which program gives advice on improving a person's appearance?

6   Which program deals with looking after domestic animals?

7   Which audience classification is shared by a travel show and a food show?

Read the text below and answer questions 8–14.

ST BERNADETTE FARMERS' MARKET

At the St Bernadette Farmers' Market you'll find organic vegetables, herbs, juices, wine, honey, cheese, smoked meat and fish, free-range eggs and more – all sold directly by the growers. Get the best of Palmerston's seasonal fresh produce right on St Bernadette's doorstep.

It's certainly not your average shopping expedition. Farmers show up from across the state. There's an abundance of fresh, seasonal and organic fruit and veggies, and also eggs, meat, organic and sourdough breads, berries, chutneys, jams and so much more.

Unlike anything else in the Palmerston area, St Bernadette Farmers' Market brings a slice of rural life to the city and provides a Saturday morning food-gathering experience like no other. All goods are grown and made by those who sell them, and the quality of produce is their main priority.

The market is plastic bag free, so bring your own baskets, bags and trolleys.

When

On the first Saturday of every month

The next market is on Saturday, 5 July.

The market is open between 8.00 am and 1.30 pm.

Where

St Bernadette's Reserve (right behind Auckland Primary School), Clayton Street

More info

For more information on market operations and stalls, email the manager at joycechu@stbmarkets.com.nz

Get on our mailing list

To be added to the St Bernadette Farmers' Market mailing list and receive a reminder email a few days before each market advising what produce will be available, please email us at mailinglist@stbmarkets.com.nz

Questions 8–14

Complete the summary below.

*Choose **NO MORE THAN THREE WORDS** from the passage for each answer.*

Write your answers in boxes 8–14 on your answer sheet.

The St Bernadette Farmers' Market has a variety of delicious fresh food available. This fresh produce can be bought straight from the **8** ………………..…………… . Some people come from **9** ………………..…………… to be at the market. The most important thing for the sellers is the **10** ……………….…………… .

Shoppers need to remember that they will not be able to get a **11** ……………..……………… at the market so they should come equipped. **12** ……………..…………… is in front of the farmers' market. People who are interested in selling something at the market should contact the **13** ………………..…………… . Those who would like to be updated about what's happening at the market should join the **14** ……………..…………… .

Read the text below and answer questions 15–22.

Job opportunities at the Belford Health Organisation

Belford Health has over 43 sites in the region of Victoria, stretching from Taunton, 65 kilometres to the north, through Mossville and down the coast as far as Westhurst and Charleston, another 50 kilometres away to the west. While Belford Health was only established in 1998, the history of the Mossville hospital dates back to 1887. Belford Health covers the full range of health services from emergency and acute to mental health, primary care, aged care and rehabilitation. It also operates five community health centres. Twenty-nine of the sites are open 24 hours a day. Belford Health provides 1,025 beds throughout its numerous sites and employs more than 4,400 staff.

Our locations

▼ The Mossville hospital has 480 beds and is located in the centre of the city of Mossville. It has a full suite of medical and surgical services and is one of the busiest hospitals in Victoria. It is well known for its burns unit and for its plastic surgery expertise.

▼ Belford Health's 300-bed St Aldan's Hospital is a general medical and surgical teaching hospital, associated with the University of Victoria and with Mossville University. It offers maternity services, and has a children's department with 85 beds.

▼ Workers in the field of aged care will appreciate the Davidson Centre, which has more than 245 beds for both low- and high-level care and for mental health patients.

▼ Major specialist consultant services are also found in smaller regional centres throughout the area, so that the needs of the community are fulfilled regardless of distance from Mossville.

Working conditions

▼ We offer a variety of working hours for staff, including full-time, part-time and casual. 32% of our staff are employed on a part-time basis.

▼ We provide flexible working options such as rostered days off.

▼ Salary packaging is available.

▼ Extensive staff education and development programs are provided so that staff may increase their expertise and keep up to date with new developments in medical care.

▼ All Belford Health staff are paid according to standard salary scales for health workers, and salary scales are reviewed annually.

Questions 15–19

*Complete each sentence with the correct ending, **A–H**, below.*

*Write the correct letter, **A–H**, in boxes 15–19 on your answer sheet.*

15   The Mossville hospital is

16   The general medical hospital is

17   Aged care staff work

18   St Aldan's Hospital is

19   Belford Health staff are

A to the east and north of Mossville.

B set up to care for mothers and babies.

C a busy teaching and research hospital.

D in the Davidson Centre.

E able to undertake training programs.

F linked with two universities.

G in the middle of the city.

H appreciative of generous salaries.

Questions 20–22

Complete the sentences below.

*Choose **ONE NUMBER ONLY** from the passage for each answer.*

Write your answers in boxes 20–22 on your answer sheet.

20   More than .... medical facilities in the Mossville area belong to Belford

Health.

21   While the company itself was more recently founded, the central hospital was founded in

....

22   The organisation is able to cater for a total of .... patients at any one time.

Read the text below and answer questions 23–28.

Applicants for teaching positions at Holden Grammar School

INFORMATION SHEET

Qualifications

Teachers employed at Holden Grammar School are required by State law to be fully trained by a recognised and accredited institution that offers a three-year, full-time Diploma of Teaching. This is the minimum qualification required but other, higher qualifications may be accepted provided that they include a minimum of 12 weeks supervised teaching practice in a recognised primary or secondary school. Applicants for positions in this school should note, however, that a Master's or PhD degree in Education that does not include teaching practice is not acceptable.

General duties

Holden Grammar School is a recognised girls' and boys' private school with approximately 800 students at secondary level. All teachers have additional responsibilities such as sports training, general playground supervision, class or group mentoring and attendance at various functions including parent–teacher nights, staff meetings and curriculum meetings.

Dress policy

Holden Grammar School has a dress code for the students, who are required to wear the school uniform while attending class and at official school functions. While there is no dress code for staff, they are expected to dress conservatively rather than informally while carrying out their duties; for example, wearing jeans and a T-shirt is unacceptable on school premises, although at school camps such informal clothing is acceptable.

Salary

Salaries paid by the school reflect those in the State salary scale, with extra allowances paid for additional responsibilities as well as for years of teaching experience. Those colleagues involved in sports training will be provided with suitable clothing and equipment.

Senior staff

Senior Heads of Department may be responsible for assisting the Principal in a variety of ways, such as interviewing prospective applicants for teaching, advising the Principal in discussions with parents, or chairing or taking part in committees in various aspects of school management.

Teachers' programs

All teachers in Years 11 and 12 will be required to make themselves available to teach at least one other subject aside from their major subject area. Middle school teachers will be expected to be able to teach in three subject areas, although this will not always be required.

Funding

Although Holden Grammar School is a private school it is not financially linked to any religion or other type of society. Students' educational costs are met only by the fees charged to parents, government grants and gifts from friends of the school. The school does not seek to make a commercial profit. Any financial surplus at the end of the year is used to improve the various facilities of the school.

Questions 23–28

Do the following statements agree with the information given in the text?

In boxes 23–28 on your answer sheet write

TRUE   if the statement agrees with the information

FALSE   if the statement contradicts the information

NOT GIVEN   if there is no information on this

23   All teachers at Holden Grammar School must have completed studies with a practical component.

24   Teachers may choose which sports training they wish to be involved in.

25   The same dress requirements apply to teachers whenever they are with students.

26   Higher salaries are paid to teachers who have been working for a long time.

27   Teachers of Years 11 and 12 may confine their teaching to their specialised fields.

28   The amount of government funding is greater than private donations to the school.

Read the text below and answer questions 29–40.

GOLD

Gold has a long and complex history. From its first discovery, it has symbolized wealth and power. Gold has caused obsession in men and nations, destroyed some cultures and given control to others.

Archaeological digs suggest the use of gold began in the Middle East where the first known civilizations began. The oldest pieces of gold jewelry were found in the tomb of Queen Zer and that of Queen Pu-abi of Ur in Sumeria in a find from the third millennium BC. Gold was also favored by the Egyptian pharaohs. Over the centuries, most of their tombs were raided, but the tomb of the pharaoh Tutankhamen was discovered undisturbed by modern archaeologists. Inside, the largest collection of gold and jewelry in the world was found. They uncovered a gold coffin whose quality showed the advanced state of Egyptian craftsmanship and goldworking. The Persian Empire, in what is now Iran, also made frequent use of gold as part of the religion of Zoroastrianism. Persian goldwork is most famous for its animal art, which was modified after the Arabs conquered the area in 642 AD.

When Rome began to flourish, the city attracted talented gold artists who created a wide variety of gold jewelry. The use of gold in Rome was later expanded to include household items and furniture in the homes of the very wealthy. During the reign of emperor Constantine (306–337 AD), the citizens of Rome wore necklaces that contained coins with the image of the emperor. As Christianity spread through the European continent, Europeans ceased burying their dead with jewelry. As a result, few gold items survive from the Middle Ages, except those of royalty and items belonging to churches.

In the Americas, the skill of pre-Columbian cultures in the use of gold was highly advanced long before the arrival of the Spanish.

Native goldsmiths had mastered most of the techniques known by their European contemporaries when the Spanish arrived in 1492. They were adept at methods of working gold into items of jewellery. The Spanish conquerors melted down most of the gold that they took from the peoples of this region, and the remaining examples of pre-Columbian jewelry still found originate from modern excavations of grave sites. The greatest deposits of gold from these times were found in the Andes mountains and in Colombia.

During the frontier days of the United States, news of the discovery of gold in a region could result in thousands of new settlers, many risking their lives to find gold. Gold rushes occurred in many of the Western States, the most famous being in California at Sutter's Mill. Elsewhere in the world, gold rushes happened in Australia around the town of Ballarat in 1851, and later in South Africa near Johannesburg, and in Canada in 1897.

The rise of the gold standard was originally meant to stabilize the global economy, dictating that a nation must limit its issued currency to the amount of gold it held in reserve. Great Britain was the first country to adopt the gold standard in 1821, followed in the 1870s by much of the rest of Europe. The system remained in effect until the end of the First World War, after which the United States was the only country still keeping to the gold standard. After the war, countries were allowed to keep their reserves in major currencies instead of gold. The onset of the Great Depression marked the end of the US export of gold in the 1930s. By 1950, the US dollar had largely replaced gold in international trade.

While gold is an ancient metal of wealth, commerce and beauty, it also has a number of unique properties that make it invaluable in

continued ▶

industry. These properties include resistance to corrosion, electrical conductivity, ductility and malleability, infrared (heat) reflectivity and thermal conductivity.

Gold's superior electrical conductivity, malleability and resistance to corrosion have made it vital to the manufacture of components used in a wide range of electrical products and equipment, including computers, telephones, mobile phones and home appliances. Gold also has extraordinarily high reflective powers that are relied upon in the shielding that protects spaceships and satellites from solar radiation, and in industrial and medical lasers that use gold-coated reflectors to focus light energy. Because gold is biologically inactive, it has become a vital tool for medical research and is even used in the direct treatment of arthritis and other intractable diseases.

The demand for gold in industry is steady and growing. The supply of gold from government stores and from mining operations is limited and will remain so. Demand from investors who want to posses this precious metal is steady, and increases during periods of world crisis or instability. The result is a market with a very positive potential. Investment gold is therefore an excellent hedge against inflation, and protects earnings for the future. Modern investors can invest in gold in the traditional way – by purchasing gold in the form of bars or coins – or they can trade in gold electronically, or by investing in gold mining or refining companies.

Questions 29–34

Complete the summary below.

Choose **NO MORE THAN THREE WORDS** *from the passage for each answer.*

Write your answers in boxes 29–34 on your answer sheet.

Since gold was first found, it has represented prosperity and **29** .... It has

been responsible for the rise and fall of cultures and has led to **30** .... in

individuals and countries. Archaeologists believe that **31** .... was the first

place where gold was first used. The pharaohs were very fond of gold and the fine artistry of ancient

Egypt could be seen in a **32** .... made of gold. **33** ....

is a distinctive feature of gold craftsmanship from Persia. In Rome, gold jewellery adorned with

pictures of the **34** .... was worn.

Questions 35–40

*Choose the correct letter **A**, **B**, **C** or **D**.*

Write your answers in boxes 35–40 on your answer sheet.

35 When the Spanish came to the Americas

    A   they found necklaces to take back to Spain.

    B   they discovered large quantities of gold in its raw form.

    C   the lcoal goldsmiths refused to teach their craft.

    D   the indigenous people were already practised in working with gold.

36 The value of gold shielding rests upon its

    A   capacity to conduct electricity.

    B   ability to cast off radiation.

    C   use in the transfer of energy.

    D   capacity to withstand a vacuum.

37 Gold has many uses in the field of medicine because

    A   it does not react organically.

    B   it a common metal.

    C   it can treat arthritis.

    D   it is highly reflective.

38 The interest in gold for investment grows

    A   when there is an international emergency.

    B   because the industrial uses of gold are increasing.

    C   when the supply from mining is low.

    D   because the reserves of stored gold are finite.

39 Gold for investment purposes is popular because

    A   there are many different ways in which people can invest in gold.

    B   it can guard against financial uncertainties in the future.

    C   the industry has continued to move with the times.

    D   its value does not decrease.

40 The most suitable title for the reading passage on gold would be

    A   'The discovery and traditional properties of gold'.

    B   'The history of gold in the Western world'.

    C   'The industrial and medical uses of gold'.

    D   'A history of gold and its uses'.

READING ANSWER SHEET

Pencil must be used to complete this sheet.

1			**21**		
2			**22**		
3			**23**		
4			**24**		
5			**25**		
6			**26**		
7			**27**		
8			**28**		
9			**29**		
10			**30**		
11			**31**		
12			**32**		
13			**33**		
14			**34**		
15			**35**		
16			**36**		
17			**37**		
18			**38**		
19			**39**		
20			**40**		
				Total	

This page may be photocopied by the original purchaser.

Writing

What is in the writing module?

Format of questions	
Task 1	You are asked to write a letter responding to a situation. You may have to give a description or an explanation, express a wish for something you want, invite someone, or make a request.
Task 2	You are asked to write a response to an opinion or argument, perhaps expressing your own opinion on the topic.
Time allowed	60 minutes It is suggested that you spend approximately 20 minutes on Task 1 and 40 minutes on Task 2. Your grade on Task 2 is worth twice as much as your grade on Task 1.
Number of words required	
Task 1	150 words minimum
Task 2	250 words minimum
Writing skills	See detailed guidelines in *Focusing on IELTS: Reading and Writing Skills* (Lindeck, Greenwood and O'Sullivan 2011). Task 1: pages 121–42 Task 2: pages 170–206

Tips for doing the Writing Test

Timing

▼ You have a total of 60 minutes – watch the time carefully.

▼ Allocate about 20 minutes for Task 1 and 40 minutes for Task 2.

▼ You can do Task 1 or Task 2 first.

▼ Task 2 is worth more marks than Task 1.

▼ Just before the hour is up, spend a few minutes checking your writing.

▼ If you find a mistake, cross out the error and write the correct version above it.

▼ Your writing needs to be clear so that it is easy for the examiner to understand what you have written.

▼ When preparing for the test, do the writing tasks under test conditions: write by hand, keep to the time limit and do not use dictionaries.

Make a plan

▼ Make a brief plan before you start writing.

▼ You can write your plan on the question sheet.

▼ A couple of minutes spent on a plan will help you produce a more logically structured answer that deals with all parts of the question.

Answer the question

▼ Pay careful attention to the question.

▼ Write an answer that is relevant to the task.

▼ Read the question several times while writing your answer to remind yourself what it is about.

▼ Make sure that you keep to the point.

▼ Answer each part of the question.

Paragraphs

▼ Task 1 should usually contain at least three paragraphs.

▼ Task 2 should usually contain at least five paragraphs.

▼ Make the beginning of a new paragraph clear by indenting or by leaving a blank line between paragraphs.

▼ Each paragraph covers a separate point.

▼ Use whole sentences – notes or bullet points are not acceptable.

Length

▼ If you do not write at least the minimum number of words for each task, you will be penalised.

▼ Do not waste time during the test counting the number of words you have written.

▼ While practising, you can get an idea of approximately how long an essay of 150 or 250 words is.

▼ Do not copy the question in your answer – a copied question is not included in the overall word count.

▼ You do not get a better score for writing an answer that is much longer than the minimum requirement.

Task 1

▼ You have to write a letter describing a situation or problem of some kind.

▼ You have to give or request information and perhaps make a suggestion or say what you will do.

▼ You may express a viewpoint or your wishes concerning the matter.

▼ You must deal with all the bullet points in the question.

▼ If you do not fully answer the question, you will be penalised.

▼ You need to use the form of a letter, though you do not need to write your address or the date.

▼ At the beginning of the letter you need to write *Dear* ..., (for example, *Dear Tim* or *Dear Anne* or *Dear Sir*).

▼ At the end of the letter you need to write an appropriate closing phrase, such as *Yours sincerely* or *Yours truly* or *Best wishes*.

Task 2

▼ Task 2 essays are longer and may require more thought and planning.

▼ You may have to argue for and/or against something, give your own opinion, describe a situation in your country or say what you think should be done.

▼ Your introductory paragraph should usually outline your answer to the specific question.

▼ Your main body paragraphs should expand on these thoughts, covering one main idea in each paragraph.

▼ You should develop the ideas and give some details and/or examples.

▼ Make sure that your answer is relevant to the actual question that has been asked – if the question contains the word 'environment', for example, do not simply start writing about pollution or climate change.

- ▼ Try to vary the length and structure of your sentences.

- ▼ Do not experiment with very long sentences if you are not sure of your grammar.

- ▼ Try to use a wide range of vocabulary.

- ▼ Your final paragraph can be quite short and may summarise your answer, but do not simply repeat the words of your opening paragraph.

Assessment criteria

In each task you are assessed using the following four criteria: answering the question, coherence and cohesion, vocabulary, and grammar.

Answering the question

The examiner will assess to what extent you have answered all parts of the question in the correct format and how much detail you have provided.

In Task 1 you need to explain why you are writing the letter, and the tone needs to be consistent and appropriate. For example, if you are writing a letter to a friend, you would use an informal, friendly style, whereas if you are writing a letter of complaint to a company or government body, you would use more formal vocabulary and a formal structure.

In Task 2 you need to provide relevant, detailed arguments and ideas. There should be a concluding paragraph.

Coherence and cohesion

Your answer needs to flow so that it is a structured piece of writing rather than just a number of unconnected sentences. This means that you need to use sequencers, referencing, substitution and linking devices, and you need to arrange the information logically. There must be a sufficient number of paragraphs and you should start a new paragraph for each separate point.

Vocabulary

You should try to use a range of vocabulary that is appropriate to the type of writing, and to demonstrate a capacity to paraphrase. Correct spelling is important. You can use either British English or American English spelling, but it should be consistent. It is not a good idea to use a lot of very long and unusual words, as it is easy to use them wrongly.

Grammar

Your writing is assessed on the variety of grammatical structures used and how accurate they are. You can get a higher score if you use complex structures with subordinate clauses rather than only short, simple sentences. Punctuation is assessed as part of grammar.

Writing Test 1

Writing Task 1

You should spend about 20 minutes on this task.

You normally travel to work by train, but the railway timetable has been changed and the train you usually took no longer stops at your station.

Write a letter to the railway authorities. In your letter:

- *introduce yourself and say how you used to travel by train*
- *describe the problems the new timetable causes you*
- *say what you want the railway authorities to do.*

Write at least 150 words.

You do **NOT** need to write any addresses.

Begin your letter as follows:

Dear Sir/Madam,

Writing Task 2

You should spend about 40 minutes on this task.

Write about the following topic:

> *Some people think that the government should pay one of the parents of very young children to stay at home to look after their children.*
>
> *What do you think would be the advantages and disadvantages of this policy?*

Give reasons for your answer and include any relevant examples from your own knowledge or experience.

Write at least 250 words.

After you have completed this practice test, check pages 166–7 of the answer key for a sample response.

Writing Test 2

Writing Task 1

You should spend about 20 minutes on this task.

> *You recently moved to a new address. You want to tell a friend who lives in another city about your new home.*
>
> *Write a letter to your friend. In your letter:*
> - *explain why you moved*
> - *describe your new home*
> - *invite your friend to visit you.*

Write at least 150 words.

You do **NOT** need to write any addresses.

Begin your letter as follows:

Dear ...,

Writing Task 2

You should spend about 40 minutes on this task.

Write about the following topic:

> *People should be encouraged to do leisure activities such as mountain climbing or sailing alone round the world, even though these activities may be dangerous, because this will help to develop their courage and confidence.*
>
> *To what extent do you agree or disagree with this opinion?*

Give reasons for your answer and include any relevant examples from your own knowledge or experience.

Write at least 250 words.

After you have completed this practice test, check pages 168–9 of the answer key for a sample response.

Writing Test 3

Writing Task 1

You should spend about 20 minutes on this task.

You are going to travel abroad for two months and while you are away a friend would like to live in your apartment. Write to the owner of the apartment explaining the situation.

In your letter:

- *explain that you are going to travel abroad*
- *describe your friend and say why he/she would be a good tenant*
- *ask whether the owner will agree to this.*

Write at least 150 words.

You do **NOT** need to write any addresses.

Begin your letter as follows:

Dear Sir/Madam,

Writing Task 2

You should spend about 40 minutes on this task.

Write about the following topic:

Some people believe that having a pet such as a cat or a dog helps old people to have a more enjoyable life and to stay healthier.

How do you think old people benefit from having a pet?

Do you think there are any problems in old people having a pet?

Give reasons for your answer and include any relevant examples from your own knowledge or experience.

Write at least 250 words.

After you have completed this practice test, check pages 169–70 of the answer key for a sample response.

Writing Test 4

Writing Task 1

You should spend about 20 minutes on this task.

You recently changed jobs, and you want to tell a person who you used to work with about your change of job.

Write a letter to that person. In your letter:

- *describe your new job*
- *explain whether you think it was a good idea to change jobs*
- *suggest that you meet again soon.*

Write at least 150 words.

You do **NOT** need to write any addresses.

Begin your letter as follows:

Dear ...,

Writing Task 2

You should spend about 40 minutes on this task.

Write about the following topic:

> *In some countries people who have high incomes pay very high taxes.*
>
> *What are the advantages and disadvantages of this for individuals and for the country as a whole?*

Give reasons for your answer and include any relevant examples from your own knowledge or experience.

Write at least 250 words.

After you have completed this practice test, check pages 170–1 of the answer key for a sample response.

Speaking

What is in the speaking module?

This test is the same for Academic and General Training candidates.

Time allowed	11 to 14 minutes
Procedure	The Speaking Test is normally the last part of the IELTS test. It is conducted as a face-to-face interview and is recorded.
The format	There are three parts to the test. Each part has a different format.
	Part 1: Introduction and interview (4 to 5 minutes) First the examiner greets you and checks your ID. Then the examiner asks you questions about yourself, for example, about where you live, your work, study, interests and other familiar topics. These topics may include matters such as food, travel and entertainment.
	Part 2: Individual long turn (3 to 4 minutes) You have to talk about a topic connected to your own experience. The examiner hands you a card with the topic on it and gives you some paper and a pencil to make notes. You have one minute to read the card and think about what you're going to say, then the examiner asks you to talk for one to two minutes. The examiner tells you when to stop. After you have finished, the examiner might ask you one or two follow-up questions.
	Part 3: Discussion (4 to 5 minutes) The examiner engages you in a discussion about topics that have the same general theme as Part 2, but the questions are of a general rather than a personal nature. Some questions are concrete, others are more abstract. For detailed explanation see *Focusing on IELTS: Listening and Speaking Skills* (Thurlow and O'Sullivan 2011) pages 65–76.
Speaking strategies and skills	See detailed guidelines in 'Speaking strategies and skills', *Focusing on IELTS: Listening and Speaking Skills* (Thurlow and O'Sullivan 2011), pages 77–126.

Tips for doing the Speaking Test

In the Speaking Test the examiner has to follow a standard structure and ask a series of questions. It is an opportunity for you to show how good your spoken English is, so it's better to give detailed answers rather than very short answers. It's normal to feel nervous during the interview, so you don't need to tell the examiner that you're nervous or that you need a good score. The topics used in all parts of the Speaking Test are chosen so that the average person can talk about them without much difficulty.

Part 1

▼ Listen carefully to the questions and try to give relevant answers.

▼ If you don't understand a question, you can ask the examiner to repeat it.

▼ If there's a word you don't understand, you can ask the examiner to explain it.

Part 2

▼ Listen as the examiner reads out your topic.

▼ If you don't like the topic that you are given or you don't know much about it, you still have to talk about it.

▼ Read the candidate's card carefully.

▼ Determine whether you are being asked to talk about something that happened in the past, or about a situation now or something that may happen in the future.

▼ Use the minute to prepare by making a few notes about what you are going to say.

▼ Use the appropriate tenses for the context.

▼ While you talk, you can look at your own notes and the candidate's card to remind yourself of what you wanted to say.

▼ Don't worry about the time – the examiner will stop you after the two minutes are up.

Part 3

▼ After the monologue of the individual long turn in Part 2, the examiner will ask you a series of questions.

▼ If you don't understand a question, you can ask the examiner to clarify it.

▼ Your English is being assessed, not your knowledge.

▼ If you say things that are not true or not factually correct, you will not be penalised.

Assessment criteria

You are assessed on four criteria: fluency and coherence, vocabulary, grammar and pronunciation.

Fluency and coherence

▼ Try to keep speaking without a lot of hesitation or repetition.

▼ Connect sentences and ideas so that there is a smooth flow to what you say and it makes sense.

Vocabulary

▼ Use vocabulary accurately, flexibly and appropriately.

▼ Use paraphrase and idiomatic language.

▼ You are not expected to speak in a formal style or to use academic vocabulary.

▼ You can gain a higher score if you go beyond basic vocabulary and can use some less common words and expressions correctly.

Grammar

▼ Use a variety of grammatical structures accurately.

▼ You can get a higher score by using complex sentences with subordinate clauses rather than only short, simple sentences.

Pronunciation

▼ Speak clearly and use features of spoken language (stress, intonation and rhythm) to communicate effectively.

▼ This includes pronunciation at the level of individual words and of sentences.

▼ If you speak very quickly, it may be difficult to understand you at times, which will affect your mark.

▼ If you speak very slowly or hesitate a lot, there will not be sufficient connected speech for the features of good pronunciation to appear.

Sample speaking tests

In this section full transcripts are provided for the three complete recorded **sample speaking tests** on the CD that accompanies this book. The topics and questions used in these recorded sample tests are given first, so you can also practise giving your own answers to these questions and compare your answers to those given by the recorded candidates. An analysis of the performance of each of the three candidates can be found in the answer key at the back of the book.

The recorded sample speaking tests are followed by six complete **practice speaking tests**. The questions only for these tests are on the CD. For these practice tests, you should listen and pause after each question so you can practise answering it. If you work with a study partner, your study partner can read the questions for you to answer. You may find it useful to record your own answers and then listen to and analyse your own performance.

Remember that in the IELTS test, the examiner will sometimes ask you 'follow-up' questions after you have responded – questions such as 'Why?' or 'Why not?' or 'Can you tell me a bit more about that?' You can hear this in the recorded sample speaking tests and see it in the transcripts. When you answer the questions in the practice speaking tests, try to give more information, as if an examiner had asked you a follow-up question.

Sample speaking test

When you listen to the recording, after you hear each question you should press 'pause' and answer the question before going on to the next question.

Part 1 Introduction and interview

Hello. Could you say your full name, please?

And can I see your passport?

Thank you. Now, in the first part of the test, I'd like to ask you some questions about yourself.

Let's talk about what you do.

Why did you decide to study English?

Is it an interesting subject to study?

Do you have plans to do further study?

Now let's go on to the topic of reading magazines.

What kinds of magazines are popular in your country?

Why do some people prefer to read magazines rather than books?

Can you learn anything from magazines?

Now I'd like to talk to you about drinks.

What are some of the most popular drinks in your country?

Are there any drinks that people have at special times?

Are there any hot drinks that you like?

What do you think are the healthiest drinks?

Part 2 Individual long turn

Now we have the second part of the Speaking Test. I'm going to give you a card about a topic and I'd like you to talk about it for one to two minutes. Before you start, you can have one minute to think about what you are going to say. If you want to, you can make some notes. Do you understand? Here's some paper and a pencil for making notes and here's your topic.

I'd like you to describe a house or an apartment that you have lived in and which you liked.

Describe a house or an apartment you have lived in and which you liked.

You should say:

       when you lived there

       how it looked inside

       what kind of area it was in

and explain why you liked living there.

All right? Remember you can talk for one to two minutes. I'll tell you when the time is up. Could you start speaking now, please?

All right, thank you.

Part 3 Discussion

All right, thank you. You've been talking about a house or an apartment you have lived in, and now I want to discuss a few more general questions connected to this. Firstly, let's look at finding a place to live.

How do people usually find a place to live in your country?

What factors do you think determine where people choose to live?

What is it like to live in an apartment compared to living in a house?

Let's now look at home ownership.

Do most people rent their homes or own their homes where you're from?

Could you compare the attitudes of someone who's renting a home and someone who owns their own home?

Should the government help people buy their own homes?

Let's now look at residential areas.

Why do you think some residential areas are more pleasant to live in than others?

Could you compare living in the centre of the city and in a suburban area?

What are the benefits of planning a residential area before people start living there?

Thank you very much. That is the end of the Speaking Test.

SPEAKING

CD 3 · Track 2

Sample speaking test: Candidate 1

Examiner: Good afternoon. Can I have your full name, please?

Candidate: Hasan Can Yuksel.

Examiner: All right, and can I see your passport, please?

Candidate: Yeah, sure.

Examiner: Thank you. That's fine. Uh, now, in the first part of the test, I'd like to ask you some questions about yourself. Um, let's talk about what you do. Are you a student, or do you have a job?

Candidate: Yeah, I am a student. I'm a student in English class.

Examiner: And why did you decide to study English?

Candidate: Er, before, because I want to study in Masters, at Masters program, er, that's why I have to study English and I have to get a IELTS score. That's why I study English.

Examiner: OK. Is it an interesting subject to study?

Candidate: Yeah. It's, er, IT, my study, er ...

Examiner: Your Masters?

Candidate: Yeah, my Masters, yeah.

Examiner: Oh, OK. And why did you decide to study IT?

Candidate: Er, because I like technology and, er, you know IT is, er, related about information and management people. That's why.

Examiner: OK. Um, now let's go on to the topic of reading magazines. Um, what kinds of magazines are popular in your country?

Candidate: Er, gossip, er, magazines popular in my country actually and, er, and also those post magazine.

Examiner: OK. So why do some people prefer to read magazines rather than books?

Candidate: Because magazines, er, has a hot topic and eh, eh, er, that's the people interested in this gossip or sports program. That's why the people prefer to magazines.

Examiner: OK. And can you learn from magazines?

Candidate: Uh, sorry?

Examiner: Can you learn from magazines?

Candidate: No, I ... I prefer to newspaper to read.

Examiner: Why's that? Why is that? Why do you prefer to read newspapers?

Candidate: Er, because, er, my first degree is economy. I have to, er, learn to economy news and that's why and I don't interest gossip and sport activities.

Examiner: So, do you often read magazines?

Candidate: No.

Examiner:	OK.
Candidate:	No I don't read often.
Examiner:	OK. Um, now I'd like to talk to you, um, about drinks.
Candidate:	Yeah.
Examiner:	What are some of the most popular drinks in your country?
Candidate:	In my country is mopular, eh, most popular drinks is special Turkish drinks is alcohol, eh, it's, er, we call draku. It's, er, has, er, high level of alcohol inside.
Examiner:	Uh-huh, OK.
Candidate:	And beer, also.
Examiner:	Right. Are there any drinks that people have at special times?
Candidate:	Um, yes, birthdays or some celebrates, er, New Year celebrates, people prefer to drink.
Examiner:	Mm. Right. OK. Um, are there any hot drinks that you like?
Candidate:	Yeah, we, er, drink a tea but hot. Er, we prefer to hot tea, not iced tea and coffee as well.
Examiner:	Mm. OK. And, um, what do you think are the healthiest drinks? What do you think are the healthiest drinks?
Candidate:	Er, I like healthiest drinks, especially milk, um, yeah, er, yeah, just milk I think.
Examiner:	OK. All right. Well, now we have the second part of the Speaking Test. I'm going to give you a card about a topic, and I'd like you to talk about it for one to two minutes. Before you start, you can have one minute to think about what you are going to say, and if you want to, you can make some notes.
Candidate:	Mm hm.
Examiner:	Do you understand?
Candidate:	Yeah, I understand.
Examiner:	All right. So here's some paper and a pencil for making notes, and here's your topic.
Candidate:	Thank you.
Examiner:	I'd like you to describe a house or an apartment you have lived in and which you liked.

You can see the candidate's card for this speaking test on page 105.

Candidate:	Er, I wanna …
Examiner:	All right, so remember, you can talk for one to two minutes, and I'll tell you when the time is up. Right? Can you start speaking now, please?
Candidate:	OK. I will describe my, er, apartments in my country. Eh, it's, ah, ooh, my apartments has a, er, eight level, eight floor, and we lived in, er, seventh floor,

and I like, I like it because this apartments has, er, a lot of, er, er, some, er, we have a swimming pool and tennis courts, er, it has a lots of facility, er, for, er, social life and, er, I used to, er, I used to both of them. And, um, we, er, our apartments is, er, in Istanbul in Turkey, and, er, it's, er, it has a, er, our home flat, er, has, er, three rooms and, er, has a huge, really huge kitchen and my mum actually, er, like it, like the huge kitchen and, um, it's, er, very close to our shop and we can go by walking. It's, er, and, er, this is, er, this house, this apartments, er, a little, er, suburb, little far to centre in Istanbul, but I like it, it's not crowded. Our area's so quiet and the people is, er, elite people and, er, our neighbours also is, er, kind peoples and we talking to neighbours, er, always and, er, we visit each other forgot my neigh … our neighbours and, er, we have a good relation in our apartments.

Examiner: So, is your home similar to most other places in the area?

Candidate: Er, little different, not similar, little different, a little, er, high quality than the others.

Examiner: And has that area changed since you first lived there?

Candidate: Yeah, it's changed because, er, this, er, building, this apartments, er, built, er, several years ago, maybe, er, seven years ago, and after the finished this apartments, it's changed, this area is changed.

Examiner: All right, thank you. You've been talking, um, about a house or an apartment you have lived in, and now I want to discuss a few more general questions connected to this. Um, firstly, let's look at finding a place to live. Um, how do people usually find a place to live in your country?

Candidate: Er, the people, er, find a quiet place to live in my country because the centre is so crowded and so noisy. The people prefer to quiet place.

Examiner: And what other factors do you think determine where people choose to live?

Candidate: Others, er, I think main factor is, er, their jobs, the people's jobs because it's, er, really big problem in the, er, metropol cities, er, the traffic you know, lots of cars and crowded. You must go early every time and this is other factor for choose their apartments.

Examiner: Right. All right, and can you compare for me, say, in Istanbul, um, living, what it's like to live in an apartment compared to living in a house?

Candidate: Ah yeah. Er, my apartment has, I like my apartments, but, er, I, er, wants to live, er, er, good view, has a good view apartments and maybe he, er, I … when I look at the window I can see a ocean or river or like this or lake.

Examiner: But, generally, what are the differences between living in an apartment and living in a house, say, in a city like Istanbul?

Candidate: Ah, it's too different, it's too different. Er, in Istanbul the people generally live in the apartment, but if you live in the houses, er, you have, er, not good relationships for their neighbours. Because it's different in Turkey. Er, if you live apartment you can get easily, er, a friend and yeah it's advantage for make a good relationships.

Examiner: OK. Um, let's now look at, um, home ownership. Um, do most people rent their homes or own their homes where you're from?

Candidate: In Turkey, eh, most people, eh, buy a home, not rent because this, er, our home prices is not, er, high. Is quite cheap, and you can get easily a home.

Examiner: OK.

Candidate: Because the people prefer to buy, buying a home.

Examiner: Right. So, what do you think the difference would be? What are the different attitudes between someone who's renting a home and someone who owns their own home? What's their attitude towards that home? Do you think there's a difference between a renter and an owner?

Candidate: Yes, er, there are lots of advantage or disadvantage, er, the rent or owner and if you rent a house, you can, eh, you must, er, moving, eh, you can be moved other places and always you must be ready to move, yes. But if you own the house, the, er, one disadvantages own the house, you can, you live, always you live the same place and you never change in your tirement, and all the same, all the people the same.

Examiner: Right.

Candidate: But if you're a renter you can change and you can get new friends, you can see a new place.

Examiner: Right. Right, well let's now look at, um, residential areas. Um, why do you think it is that some areas, some residential areas, are more pleasant to live in than others?

Candidate: More?

Examiner: More pleasant to live in.

Candidate: Er, because the er, residence, residential areas, is er, uh er, it's not, er, really it's not in Turkey, it's not, er, maybe it's, er, for, er, develop, developed countries, it's not, er, for developing countries, 'cause it's different. Um, actually we have no, er, we have no one centre, and we have no residence areas. All this you can go and see, you can stay.

Examiner: Right, but I guess is one area nicer than another area?

Candidate: Yeah.

Examiner: So what makes that area nicer?

Candidate: Ah nicer, er. It's yeah, it's, if it's near the centre, it's in, er, if it's, er, you can, er, get easily, er, transport, transportation, it's, er, and you can go everywhere. It's the centre like, um, it's the people prefer the like the safe areas.

Examiner: So, convenience?

Candidate: Yeah, convenience.

Examiner: Right, OK. Well, thank you very much. That's the end of the Speaking Test.

Candidate: eah, thank you.

See the answer key on pages 171–3 for an analysis of this candidate's performance.

CD 3 · Track 3

Sample speaking test: Candidate 2

Examiner: Good afternoon. Could I have your full name, please?

Candidate: Good afternoon. My full name is Luo Xiaojing; that is my Chinese name.

Examiner: All right. And can I see your passport, please?

Candidate: OK. Here you are.

Examiner: Thank you. That's fine. Now, in the first part of the test, I'd like to ask you some questions about yourself. Ah, let's talk about what you do. Are you a student or do you have a job?

Candidate: Mm, I'm a student now. I have the language course is in Macquarie and then I will going to have the Master of Commerce.

Examiner: OK. And, er, why did you decide to do a Masters of Commerce?

Candidate: Mm. Um, because I think, if I can gain the Master degree maybe I will give a good job in China. And I will have a more opportunity, uh, to get a good pay job which is more appealing.

Examiner: All right. Um, later in life do you want to study something else?

Candidate: Sorry?

Examiner: Later in life do you want to study something else?

Candidate: Yes, of course. Cause I think study is, uh, is better to me and, uh, I think, uh, I … I will continue my studies throughout my life.

Examiner: OK. Ah, now let's go on to the topic of reading magazines. Um, what kinds of magazines are popular in your country?

Candidate: Maybe the magazine about the superstars such as movie star, uh, TV star and, uh, the singer, the famous singer. Um, a lot of younger people like to see the magazine about it.

Examiner: Right. Um, why do some people prefer to read magazines rather than books?

Candidate: Mm. I think one of the reason is that in magazines, um, the people can see a lot of pictures then colourful and I think it's fantastic.

Examiner: OK. Can you learn much from magazines?

Candidate: Oh, something. You can gain some information about the magazine but I think, um, I will … I will not spend a lot of time to see the magazine.

Examiner: OK. Do you often read magazines?

Candidate: No, not often.

Examiner: Right, um, now I'd like to talk to you about drinks. Um, what are the most popular drinks in your country?

Candidate: Beer, yeah.

Examiner: Yeah, OK.

Candidate: And, uh, maybe Coca-Cola, but I dislike it. I always drink the orangey water and, uh, just drink the water.

Examiner: All right. Um, are there any drinks that people have at special times?

Candidate: Mm, yeah, uh, I think maybe in the parties such as birthday party or any, uh, celebration kind of party, the people will drink a lot of such as, uh, beer and any alcohol, alcohol water. Yeah, alcohol drink, sorry.

Examiner: Mm hm. All right. Um, are there any hot drinks you like?

Candidate: No I don't like.

Examiner: OK and, uh, what do you think are the healthiest drinks?

Candidate: Mm. In my country a lot of people believe that, um, a little drink is better to your health, but I'm not sure because I think the men is always drink a lot and they cannot control, so I think drink is lot to their body.

Examiner: Right. Now we have the second part of the Speaking Test. I'm going to give you a card about a topic, and I'd like you to talk about it for one to two minutes. Before you start, you can have one minute to think about what you are going to say, and if you want to, you can make some notes. Do you understand?

Candidate: Yes.

Examiner: All right. So here is some paper and a pencil for making notes, and here's your topic. I'd like you to describe a house or an apartment you've lived in and which you liked.

You can see the candidate's card for this speaking test on page 105.

Examiner: All right? So remember, you can talk for one to two minutes. I'll tell you when the time is up. Could you start speaking now, please?

Candidate: Yeah, now I will describe a house to you. Um, once I have been to Sydney I live in a big, very big house. The house has in Willoughby. You know Willoughby is quite far from the Macquarie and I like … I like the house very much because it's, it's very beautiful. The house is very big. There are six bedroom and two toilets, hm, a kitchen, a living room, uh, and a, a very big parking room. I think it's very big, um, because in, in China my apartment is quite small so I fe … I always fix stress when I live in it. Mm, ah, ah, after, after the courses I always go to, go to my house, I prefer to stay in my bedroom instead of go outside because, uh, I have a little friend and I think, uh, the house is quite comfortable. Mm, uh, of, of course I have three, three housemate. Most of them come from China. We always chat but, uh, one of the problem is that we always chat with Chinese. I think that is not good enough to me. Uh, in a word I like the house and I think it's beautiful, clear, large and, uh, it's very comfortable, so I think it's better for me.

Examiner: So is that home similar to other places in the area?

Candidate: Sorry?

Examiner: Is that home similar to other places in the area?

Candidate: Mm, no, maybe not.

Examiner: OK. All right. Well thank you very much.

Candidate: Oh, thanks.

Examiner: You've been talking about a house or an apartment you have lived in, and now I want to discuss a few more general questions connected to this. Firstly, let's look at finding a place to live. Um, how do people usually find a place to live in your country?

Candidate: In my country, always go to the, uh, look for the advertisement and to gain some information about the house. Ah, maybe you, maybe the people can use a computer, um, collect the information from the Internet or buy some new newspaper, they always have some information about it. Ah, of course there are agents about just, uh, work for the, the rent, so I think it's quite easy for a person who want to have, who want to have, who want to have looking for a house.

Examiner: All right. So what factors do you think determine where people choose to live?

Candidate: Mm, I think most of, most of the important reason is comfortable and the price and the convenient. Yeah.

Examiner: Right. And, um, how would you compare, then, living in an apartment and living in a house?

Candidate: Mm, when I in China I live in the apartment, it's quite small, mm, and, ah, I will feel, um, it's not as comfortable as the house. However, uh, in my, in my a …, a …, sorry, apartment, I, I never find any insect because I live in the fifth floor of the building, the building quite high and, uh, higher world than when I lived in the house. Uh, sometime they can find the insect climbing to my house. I'm afraid of it.

Examiner: All right. Well, now let's look at home ownership. Um, do most people in your country rent their home or do they own their own home?

Candidate: Mm, if they have house or apartment, uh, most of people prefer to live in his own house because the, the rent of the house is quite expensive, especially in Shanghai and Beijing and in other big cities. Mm, I think the people should not put some money to rent a house if he had his own house. That's not economic.

Examiner: So what do you think is the difference in attitudes towards a house if you are a renter or you are an owner of that house? Do you think their attitudes towards their homes are different?

Candidate: Towards?

Examiner: Um, no, do you think an attitude of a renter, um, of a house compared to the attitude of an owner of the house is different?

Candidate: Oh, of course it's different. If I have my own house, I lived in it and I feel, oh, that it, that belongs to me. And I think I have a family, um, but if I live in the house just rent from somebody, I think I'm always worried maybe I will have to move another house.

Examiner: Right.

Candidate: I think that it quite different.

Examiner: So how does that affect how they treat the house?

Candidate: Mm, treat?

Examiner: Um, how, how they, um, how they treat that house. So, do you think that they think of the house in a better way or a worse way, if they are a renter?

Candidate: Yeah, uh, I think the people can compare with others. If I have rent a house and I lived it for a, for a long time, maybe I think, oh, it's OK to me, but when I look, um, with it to my friend, maybe I will find out that his house is better to me, so I will all think maybe I will have to looking for another house.

Examiner: OK. Lastly, let's look at residential areas. Um, do you think that it's better to live in the city or that it's better to live in a suburban area?

Candidate: Mm. I think the both benefit and, uh, disadvantages to live in the city or the countryside. Uh, in the city the life will become very convenient and it's very easy for you to go out for shopping and visit your friend and, uh, check bars to any place, but I think the, maybe the environment is not good enough and the traffic is bad too. If you want to go out or go to work, go to university, you'll find that the traffic always block, it will waste a lot of time. Mm. However, if the person live in countryside, uh, and the life is very leisure, but I think you maybe you will feel lonely. Yeah, nobody can try to reach you, nobody can tell, can take care of you. You just live by yourself, and maybe you just stay at home and watch the TV and, uh, call your friend. I think, uh, it's bad for the young people.

Examiner: OK. Well, thank you very much. That's the end of the Speaking Test.

Candidate: Thanks.

See the answer key on page 173–4 for an analysis of this candidate's performance.

Sample speaking test: Candidate 3

Examiner: Hello, could you tell me your full name please?

Candidate: Robby Sedhu.

Examiner: All right and can I see your passport?

Candidate: Here is my passport.

Examiner: OK, thank you. Now, in the first part of the test I'd like to ask you some questions about yourself. Let's talk about what you do. Uh, why did you decide to study English?

Candidate: Um, because uh in in this competition of us uh you need English if you are going it helps in your career and I love to travel around the world so I think English is an international language so it will help me to communicate with people.

Examiner: OK. Is it an interesting subject to study?

Candidate: No it's not interesting subject um because you have to just learn grammar and um yes pretty boring it's not too interesting like er anything new.

Examiner: OK and do you have plans to do further study?

Candidate: Yeah I do um actually I want to become um, er nurse so I want to do that nursing course um, yeah I'm really into like um looking after people so I want to do this.

Examiner: OK now let's go on to the topic of reading magazines. What kinds of magazines are popular in your country?

Candidate: So in India people love cricket so the ... because nowadays Indian cricket players they're doing very well so the people like to buy er cricket magazines and they're reading a lot about um Indian players, yeah.

Examiner: OK why do you think some people prefer to read magazines rather than books?

Candidate: Er in books like people have to spend a lot of time to get a idea what they reading about but in magazines they can get like er, er they can get an idea about the thing what they are reading about just in a shorter um period, short period of time and in a sense like short look, quick look, yeah.

Examiner: Can you learn anything from magazines?

Candidate: Yeah you can learn a lot from magazines like um er it tells about those other products and er....

Examiner: OK that's fine, um. Now I'd like to talk to you about drinks. What are some of the most popular drinks in your country, India?

Candidate: In India actually I'm from Punjab, like, we like er traditional dishes, drink is lassi so people love to drink that lassi so it's like very nice drink and you drink it um with ice and salt so it's very popular in India.

Examiner: OK are there any drinks that people have at special times?

Candidate: Yeah there's, there are some special drinks like some um, um, er homemade alcohol that people they make them er on the wedding parties. They make at home and the drink, it's really nice the people love um love that.

Examiner: OK are there any hot drinks that you like?

Candidate: Uh I like hot drink like er hot chocolate. I really enjoy it just very dark chocolate, yeah.

Examiner: OK and finally what are the healthiest drinks, do you think?

Candidate: I think juices are the healthiest drinks and those are shakes like uh mango shake, banana shake with milk, these are the healthiest drinks.

Examiner: OK um now Robby we have the second part of the speaking test. I am going to give you a card about a topic and I'd like you to talk about it for one to two minutes. Before you start you have one minute to think about what you are going to say. If you want to, you can make some notes. Do you understand?

Candidate: Yeah, thank you.

Examiner: OK here's some paper and a pencil for making notes and here's your topic. OK I'd like you to describe a house or an apartment you have lived in and which you liked. So you have one minute to prepare.

Candidate: OK.

You can see the candidate's card for this speaking test on page 105.

Examiner: All right um remember you can talk for one to two minutes. I'll tell you when the time is up. Can you start speaking now, please?

Candidate: When I firstly came to Australia so um er I lived in Springvale er it's just like er this is a very big house, three bedroom house, I really like it, it was in very like er um peaceful area and really neat and clean. So I used to live with my friends, so I had my own room, the house was like built with um timber floor and er painted white, white and blue, so these are my favourite colours. So my room was really big and the curtains was really nice and I had that um street view from my uh from my window, I like that because there is a park on the next side of the street. So I can watch people playing football because I love football and er it was near to all the facilities like hospital, library and um supermarket and there is a park also as I just mentioned earlier, um so I love to play football it was very easy for me to just go there and just um I can just walk up for one minute and I can go there and er we had a garden also, in the front and a backyard. So I love gardening also so I had a lot of flowers and veggies at my place, some home gardens. So the house was my favorite house in my whole life er until now. So I am still looking for a house for that kind of house. So because I want to live in a very peaceful area – er just we had a one this one good thing of that house was like a separate toilet and separate wash room and separate um laundry because in Australia in Melbourne mostly um mostly in Melbourne you can't get er like different laundry facilities that was good thing about that house.

Examiner: All right, thank you Robby. You have been talking about a house or an apartment you have lived in and now I want you to discuss a few more general questions connected to this. Firstly, let's look at finding a place to live. How do people usually find a place to live in your country, India?

Candidate: Like other normal countries, in my country people also use those travel oh sorry, um those real estate agents. So these people are really helpful and they can find whatever they are looking for that's easy for them because they can tell them those people like what they are looking for and they will help to find those places and even on the other hand they can use the internet also, it is really helpful. So you can do it at home also you don't have to go and see someone else so you can find it very easily on the internet also.

Examiner: And what factors do you think determine where people choose to live?

Candidate: Like living around er um all those facilities like hospitals, library, um playgrounds and some other leisure activity centres and um dispensaries. So these kind of factors er I think determine, people should determine before er before living anywhere else.

Examiner: What is it like to live in an apartment compared to living in a house – do you think?

Candidate: Er living in a house is different than living in an apartment. So if you are living in a house, a house would be like very open side it would be big, more bigger than a apartment. So you can have a backyard also a garden also and you can you can't like, if you are living in a house you have a separate wall from your neighbours or you will have a gap between your house and the neighbour's house, so you can't hear the neighbour's cry so it will be more separate from the – from other houses. But living in er apartment is like er, um it's, living in an apartment also have some good qualities like er here it's more secure than living in a house um and you can have a view if you are living in an apartment. The building will be more taller than a house um – most stories apartments - so you can have a view of city and area wherever you are living, and you can have er fresh air if you are living in an apartment.

Examiner: OK thanks, um let's now look at home ownership. So do most people rent their homes or own their homes where you're from?

Candidate: Er in my town people actually own their own place. So because it's very expensive renting a place in um my town because it's so – we are industrial town so all those um migrant peoples are living there and it's very expensive to own uh to rent a place.

Examiner: OK, um could you compare the attitudes of someone who's renting a home and someone who owns their own home?

Candidate: People who er owns their own home. So they are very comfortable in their own place because the way you want things you can do whatever you want to do. The colour like colour wise and picture wise and the furniture wise whatever you want to do, to your place you can do. If you are renting a place it's like you, you kind of feeling like you have to move soon and you can't do this, you can't do this you, even you can't paint your room like the colour you want and the pictures you want you can't do that. And you have to look after the property a lot.

Examiner: So you're nervous if you rent a home?

Candidate: Yeah, I think so.

Examiner: OK, should the government help people to buy their own homes, do you think?

Candidate: Yeah in some like in developing countries the government should help those people who can't afford to buy a place um like um mostly those people who are living below the line, the line of poverty, so government should help them to buy a place, the government financial and er, and um help them to get a job so they can buy, so they can afford to buy a place.

Examiner: Let's now look at residential areas. Why do you think some residential areas are more pleasant to live than others?

Candidate: Some residential areas are very like er very good than others so because they er they are near to all of the facilities whatever we need in our social life like er, er activity, leisure activity centres, libraries, schools, markets and a peaceful area and some parks those are the er, um basic needs of um human beings so we need that. Yeah these places, these kinds of places are very comfortable than others.

Examiner: OK and finally, Robby, could you compare living in the centre of the city and in a suburban area?

Candidate: Living in the city is pretty congested so because the city is er, there is all those tall buildings and it's noisy and it can be a bit polluted also than suburban areas because suburban is more wider than city, you can have like a very peaceful um peaceful life in suburban areas and a bit more space so you can have your own garden and backyard but in city if you are living in an apartment it is a bit hard to get all those things, yeah.

Examiner: OK, thanks very much Robby, that is the end of the speaking test.

Candidate: Thank you.

See the answer key on pages 174–6 for an analysis of this candidate's performance.

Speaking Test 1

CD 3 • Track 5

When you listen to the recording, after you hear each question you should press 'pause' and answer the question before going on to the next question.

Part 1 Introduction and interview

Hello. Could you say your full name, please?

And can I see your passport?

Thank you. Now, in the first part of the test, I'd like to ask you some questions about yourself.

Let's talk about your work.

What job do you do?

When did you first think about doing this kind of work?

What do you like about your job?

Do you think you'll be working in this field in ten years' time?

Now let's talk about music.

What type of music did you like when you were a teenager?

Have you ever been to a live music concert?

At what times of day do you prefer to listen to music?

Do you often hear other people play music you don't like?

Next I'd like to talk about eating lunch.

What did you often eat for lunch when you were a school pupil?

Do you think lunch should be the main meal of the day?

Is it a good idea for people to have a rest after lunch?

Do you sometimes not have enough time for lunch?

Part 2 Individual long turn

Now we have the second part of the Speaking Test. I'm going to give you a card about a topic and I'd like you to talk about it for one to two minutes. Before you start, you can have one minute to think about what you are going to say. If you want to, you can make some notes. Do you understand? Here's some paper and a pencil for making notes and here's your topic.

I'd like you to describe a time when you complained about something you had paid for (for example, a restaurant meal, a product in a shop).

Describe a time when you complained about something you had paid for (e.g. a restaurant meal, a product in a shop).
You should say:

> why you complained
>
> how you complained
>
> whether it was useful to complain

and explain how you felt after you had complained.

All right? Remember you can talk for one to two minutes. I'll tell you when the time is up. Could you start speaking now, please?

Did you tell your friends about this?

Do people often complain about products and service in your country?

All right, thank you.

Part 3 Discussion

You've been talking about a time when you complained about something and now I want to discuss a few more general questions connected to this.

Firstly, let's talk about complaining.

What are some things people often complain about these days?

What is more effective – complaining by writing an email or by talking face to face with the person responsible?

Are there situations when it's better *not* to complain?

Now let's talk about being patient.

Could you describe some situations in daily life when people need to be patient?

Do you think technology such as email and mobile phones have made people less patient?

What are some benefits of being impatient?

Finally, let's talk about being satisfied in life.

Would you say most people are satisfied with their lives?

Do rich people tend to be more content than poor people?

Do you agree that, in general, humans tend to be dissatisfied rather than satisfied?

Thank you very much. That is the end of the Speaking Test.

Speaking Test 2

SPEAKING

CD 3 • Track 6

When you listen to the recording, after you hear each question you should press 'pause' and answer the question before going on to the next question.

Part 1 Introduction and interview

Hello. Could you tell me your full name, please?

And can I see your passport?

Thank you. Now, in the first part of the test, I'm going to ask you some questions about yourself.

Let's talk about what you study.

What was the last course you studied?

Did anyone encourage you to choose that course?

What was more interesting for you – attending classes or reading course materials?

Are you happy that you chose that course?

Next, let's talk about visitors to your country.

Do many people from other countries visit your country?

Have you ever met any foreign tourists in your country?

How important is tourism to the economy of your country?

Do you think tourism will increase or decrease in the next few years?

Now I'd like to talk about watching movies.

What was the last film you saw?

How often do you watch the same movie again?

Do you prefer going to the cinema in the daytime or at night?

Would you watch a whole movie on a small screen such as an iPod?

Part 2 Individual long turn

Now we come to the second part of the Speaking Test. I'm going to give you a card about a topic and I'd like you to talk about it for one to two minutes. Before you start, you can have one minute to think about what you are going to say. If you want to, you can make some notes. Do you understand? Here's some paper and a pencil for making notes and here's your topic.

I'd like you to describe an occasion when you bought a special gift or present for someone.

> Describe an occasion when you bought a special gift or present for someone.
> You should say:
>> what you bought
>> where you bought it
>> why you chose that present
> and explain how you felt when you gave the present to the other person.

All right? Remember you can talk for one to two minutes. I'll tell you when the time is up. Could you start speaking now, please?

Would you like to receive a present like that yourself?

Do you like buying presents?

All right, thank you.

Part 3 Discussion

You've been talking about a time when you bought a special gift or present for someone and now I want to discuss a few more general questions connected to this.

Firstly, let's talk about giving presents.

When do people give presents in your culture?

What kind of presents do you think adults should give to children?

Is it ever acceptable to give money as a present?

Now let's talk about receiving presents.

What are some ways people show gratitude when they receive a present?

Is there anything people should avoid doing or saying when they receive a present in your country?

Are there any situations where a person should *not* accept a gift?

Finally, let's talk about why people give and receive presents.

Would you agree or disagree with the statement that 'people sometimes give expensive presents instead of spending time with a person'?

Do you agree that, when people give presents, they usually expect something in return?

Does giving and receiving presents sometimes have negative rather than positive results?

Thank you very much. That is the end of the Speaking Test.

Speaking Test 3

CD 3 • Track 7

When you listen to the recording, after you hear each question you should press 'pause' and answer the question before going on to the next question.

Part 1 Introduction and interview

Hello. Could you tell me your full name, please?

And can I see your passport?

Thank you. Now, in the first part of the test, I'm going to ask you some questions about yourself.

Let's talk about where you live.

What made you choose the place where you live now?

How long have you lived there?

Would you say it's a good area for families to live in?

Would it be a better area to live if there were fewer people than now?

Next, let's talk about how people pay for things they buy.

How do you prefer to pay for things that you buy, in cash or by card?

When you pay cash for something, do you usually check the change that you are given?

What is the most common way of paying for things in your country?

When you go to another country, do you have problems using a different currency?

Now I'd like to talk about getting up early in the morning.

Did you like to get up early in the morning when you were a child?

What are some advantages of getting up early?

Do you feel different at the beginning of the day than at the end of the day?

What do you think is the best time to get up in the morning?

Part 2 Individual long turn

Now we come to the second part of the Speaking Test. I'm going to give you a card about a topic and I'd like you to talk about it for one to two minutes. Before you start, you can have one minute to think about what you are going to say. If you want to, you can make some notes. Do you understand? Here's some paper and a pencil for making notes and here's your topic.

I'd like you to describe a website you have used.

Describe a website you have used.
You should say:

> how you found that website
>
> what that website is about
>
> how often you access it

and explain how you feel about that website.

All right? Remember you can talk for one to two minutes. I'll tell you when the time is up. Could you start speaking now, please?

Do you think that website could be improved?

Do you use the Internet a lot?

All right, thank you.

Part 3 Discussion

You've been talking about a website you have used and now I want to discuss a few more general questions connected to this.

Firstly, let's talk about using the Internet.

What are some of the main reasons people use the Internet in your country?

Could you compare looking for information on the Internet and in a book?

How do you think the Internet might change in the future?

Now let's talk about finding reliable information.

Do you think we can generally believe what we see on the Internet?

Where can we find the most reliable reports: on the Internet, on TV or in a newspaper?

How is it possible to check whether information you receive is correct or not?

Finally, let's talk about misuse of the Internet.

What are some ways people use the Internet to trick or deceive other people?

What can governments do to try to stop Internet fraud?

Do you think that misuse of the Internet will lead to less trust between strangers in the future?

Thank you very much. That is the end of the Speaking Test.

Speaking Test 4

CD 3 • Track 8

When you listen to the recording, after you hear each question you should press 'pause' and answer the question before going on to the next question.

Part 1 Introduction and interview

Hello. Could you tell me your full name, please?

And can I see your passport?

Thank you, that's fine. Now, in the first part of the test, I'd like to ask you some questions about yourself.

Let's talk about your job.

What do you do?

When did you first start doing that job?

Do you enjoy your work?

What are the people you work with like?

Now we'll look at the topic of dancing.

Is dancing very popular in your country?

Do you and your friends prefer to dance, or to watch other people dancing?

Are there special times when people like to dance?

Do you ever go dancing?

Let's now go on to the topic of computers.

Do you often use a computer?

How are computers most helpful?

Have you ever had a problem with a computer?

Do you think it'll be possible one day to have a conversation with a computer?

Part 2 Individual long turn

Now we have the second part of the Speaking Test. I'm going to give you a card about a topic and I'd like you to talk about it for one to two minutes. Before you start, you can have one minute to think about what you are going to say. If you want to, you can make some notes. Do you understand? Here's some paper and a pencil for making notes and here's your topic.

I'd like you to describe something interesting that you are going to do in your free time.

Describe something interesting that you are going to do in your free time.

You should say:

      what it is

      when you're going to do it

      why it will be interesting

and explain how you feel about doing it.

All right? Remember you can talk for one to two minutes. I'll tell you when the time is up. Could you start speaking now, please?

Have you ever done anything like this before?

Could anything prevent you from doing it?

All right, thank you.

Part 3 Discussion

You've been talking about something interesting you are going to do and now I want to discuss a few more general questions connected to this.

Firstly, let's look at making plans.

What are some things in life that people need to plan for carefully?

Are there any important things that people cannot prepare for?

Why do you think some people don't like making plans?

Now let's talk about hopes.

In your country, what are some things that many people hope to achieve in life?

Could you compare these with the hopes and ambitions people had when your parents were young?

Why do people need to have hopes and dreams?

Finally, let's talk about attitudes to the future.

Could you compare people who are optimistic and people who are pessimistic about the future?

How does a person's attitude to the future affect their life?

Do you think that people should be optimistic about the future of the world these days?

Thank you very much. That is the end of the Speaking Test.

Speaking Test 5

When you listen to the recording, after you hear each question you should press 'pause' and answer the question before going on to the next question.

Part 1 Introduction and interview

Good afternoon. Could you tell me your full name, please?

And can I see your passport?

Thank you. Now, in the first part of the test, I'd like to ask you some questions about yourself.

Let's talk about where you live.

Could you describe the area where you live now?

How long have you lived there?

Why did you choose to live in that area?

What kind of people live in your area?

Now we'll talk about sleep.

How many hours a night do you think people need to sleep?

What do you do if you feel sleepy but you have to stay awake?

In your country, do people often have a sleep during the daytime?

How do you feel when you are woken by an alarm clock?

Now let's talk about watching television.

What kinds of TV programs do you like?

What time of day do you prefer to watch TV?

Have you ever lived in a home where there was no television?

Do you think people watch too much TV these days?

Part 2 Individual long turn

Now we come to the second part of the Speaking Test. I'm going to give you a card about a topic and I'd like you to talk about it for one to two minutes. Before you start, you can have one minute to think about what you are going to say. If you want to, you can make some notes. Do you understand? Here's some paper and a pencil for making notes and here's your topic.

I'd like you to describe a film you have seen that made an impression on you.

> Describe a film you have seen that made an impression on you.
>
> You should say:
>
> what it was about
>
> how popular it was
>
> what you thought about the actors
>
> and explain why it made an impression on you.

All right? Remember you can talk for one to two minutes. I'll tell you when the time is up. Could you start speaking now, please?

When did you last see that film?

Do you often watch films?

All right, thank you.

Part 3 Discussion

You've been talking about a film you have seen that made an impression on you and now I want to discuss a few more general questions connected to this.

Firstly, let's look at the importance of entertainment.

What kinds of entertainment are popular in your country?

Could you compare types of entertainment children like and adults like?

Why is entertainment important in people's lives?

Now let's talk about famous actors.

Why do you think people are interested in the private lives of famous actors?

In your opinion, is the amount of money earned by film stars justified?

What would it be like to be a famous actor?

Finally, let's talk about global culture.

How much influence does American culture have in your country?

What are Hollywood films like in comparison with films produced in your country?

How can a country avoid being dominated by a foreign culture?

Thank you very much. That is the end of the Speaking Test.

Speaking Test 6

CD 3 • Track 10

When you listen to the recording, after you hear each question you should press 'pause' and answer the question before going on to the next question.

Part 1 Introduction and interview

Hello. Could you tell me your full name, please?

And can I see your passport?

Thank you. Now, in the first part of the test, I'd like to ask you some questions about yourself.

Let's talk about where you come from.

Which country do you come from?

What's the best time of year to visit your country?

Are many different languages spoken in your country?

Are there any areas in your country where very few people live?

Now, let's move on to talk about light.

Do you prefer buildings with a lot of light or ones with a more shaded style?

How do you feel working or studying in a room without windows?

Do you think very bright advertising signs at night are a good idea?

Could you live without electric lights at home?

Let's go on to talk about visiting people.

Do people often visit friends in their homes in your country?

At what times or on what days do people usually visit friends?

Should you tell people you are coming before visiting them at home?

Do people ever take presents when visiting friends in your country?

Part 2 Individual long turn

Now we come to the second part of the Speaking Test. I'm going to give you a card about a topic and I'd like you to talk about it for one to two minutes. Before you start, you can have one minute to think about what you are going to say. If you want to, you can make some notes. Do you understand? Here's some paper and a pencil for making notes and here's your topic.

I'd like you to describe a river, lake or beach that you know.

Describe a river, lake or beach that you know.

You should say:

where it is

what it looks like

what people use it for

and explain whether you like it or not.

All right. Remember you can talk for one to two minutes. I'll tell you when the time is up. Could you start speaking now, please?

Do you often go to that place?

Is it a popular place for leisure activities?

All right, thank you.

Part 3 Discussion

You've been talking about a river, lake or beach that you know and now I want to ask you a few more general questions connected to this.

Firstly, let's look at holidays near water.

Could you tell me about some places near water where people like to take holidays in your country?

What are some activities people can do when they have a holiday near water?

Why do you think people often find it relaxing to be near water?

Now we'll talk about transport on water.

How important is water transportation these days?

Could you compare travelling on water and travel by road?

In the future, how important do you think travel by water will be?

And finally, let's consider water pollution.

What are some of the causes of water pollution?

What can governments do to prevent water being polluted?

What would happen if there were a global shortage of clean water?

Thank you very much. That is the end of the Speaking Test.

Transcripts

In these listening transcripts, the words that are <u>underlined</u> indicate where the answers to the questions can be found.

Listening Test 1

You will hear four different recordings and you will have to answer questions on what you hear.

There will be time for you to read the instructions and questions before the recording is played.

You will also have the opportunity to check your answers.

The recordings will be played ONCE only.

The test is in four sections. Write your answers on the question sheet as you listen. At the end of Section 4, you have ten minutes to transfer your answers onto the answer sheet, which is on page 31. When you finish, check the answers at the back of the book.

Now turn to Section 1.

Section 1

You will hear a telephone conversation between a woman who will soon move house and an employee of a telephone company.

First, you have some time to look at questions 1 to 5.

Now listen and answer questions 1 to 5.

Dan: Atlantic Telephone Company, my name is Dan. How can I help you?

Penny: Oh, hello, I'm calling because you're my telephone service provider and I'm going to be moving house next week. I need to have my phone disconnected and then I want to have it connected at the new address.

Dan: We can do that for you now over the phone, if you like.

Penny: Oh, that'd be good.

Dan: All right then. First, could you tell me your phone number?

Penny: Yes, it's 5062 7840.

The customer says the number is 5062 7840, so '5062 7840' has been written next to the example on the question paper. Now continue with questions 1 to 5.

Dan: Thank you. And is the account in your name?

Penny: Uh, yes, it is.

Dan: Could you spell your full name, please?

Penny: It's <u>Penny Ryan</u>, that's P-e-n-n-y ... R-y-a-n.

Dan: Thank you. Now, I just need to ask you a question for security purposes. I hope you don't mind, but could you tell me your date of birth, Ms Ryan?

Penny: No, I don't mind. It's the <u>24th of March 1982</u>.

Dan: Right. And do you know yet the date on which you'll be moving?

Penny: Yes, it's next Tuesday, the 16th of September.

Dan: Thank you. Now, madam, can you tell me where you'll be moving to?

Penny: My new address will be 18 King Street, <u>Blacktown</u>.

Dan: Uh-huh. I can allocate you a new telephone number now if you like, though it won't be operational till you actually have it connected.

Penny: That'd be really useful – I could tell my friends the new number even before I move.

Dan: Do you have a pen and paper handy?

Penny: Yes.

Dan: OK, your new number will be <u>7690 3275</u>.

Penny: Great.

Dan: Now, up until now you've been receiving your telephone bills once a month. As a long-standing customer, you have the option of being billed only once every three months if you like.

Penny: Oh, I'll stick with monthly bills, it just makes it easier for me to stay within my household budget.

Dan: All right then.

Before you hear the rest of the conversation, you have some time to look at questions 6 to 10.

Now listen and answer questions 6 to 10.

Dan: Now, Ms Ryan, could you tell me which type of contract you are on with Atlantic Telephone Company? Is it Home Plus, Economy Saver or Flexible Bundle?

Penny: Oh, let me think. I think I used to be on Home Plus, but then I got a mobile phone and I wasn't using my landline that much anymore, so I switched plans. That's right, I switched to Economy Saver about a year ago.

Dan: Right, thank you. Now, I'd like to tell you about a new type of contract we have. It's called the Three-In-One. If you have your landline, your mobile and the Internet connection with us, you get a 20% discount every time you pay the bill.

Penny: Oh, but with my mobile I'm using a very cheap provider, but they're not that reliable. If I do switch contracts, will I be locked in for a certain time period?

Dan: Well, that's the case with Home Plus, but with this one you're free to change again at any time without penalty.

Penny: Oh, in that case I'll switch from Economy Saver to Three-In-One.

Dan: Good. I'm sure you'll find you make real savings with that.

Penny: Oh, I just have a question about the Internet.

Dan: Yes, what do you want to know?

Penny: There are certain times when I can make unlimited downloads, like if I want to download a movie. That's from 10 pm to 6 am, isn't it?

Dan: It's a bit more restricted than that, it's from 1 am to 6 am. It turns out that the peak period of accessing large files is from 11 at night to 2 in the morning.

Penny: Oh, that's interesting, there must be a lot of night owls.

Dan: I suppose so. Now, do you mind if I ask you what's the main type of phone call you make? Any information you give me will be kept confidential, it's just information that helps us provide a better service to our customers.

Penny: Alright then, but what do you mean by 'type of phone call'?

Dan: Would you say the majority of your calls are to friends and relatives, or are they work-related, or for paying bills and so on?

Penny: Well, I started to work from home last year, so most of them were work-related, but then I didn't make enough money from that line of work, so I got a part-time job and now I mainly use the phone to call relatives. I tend to keep in contact with friends by email.

Dan: OK, thank you. Now just one more question then we'll be finished. In the years that you've been with Atlantic Telephone Company, how would you rate our service overall?

Penny: Well, initially there were a few problems, and it wasn't really satisfactory, but in general I'd say things have been mostly satisfactory. My previous service provider was very good, but they went bankrupt.

Dan: All right then, that wraps it up. Thank you very much and I hope your move goes smoothly.

Penny: Thank you.

That is the end of Section 1. You now have half a minute to check your answers.

Now turn to Section 2.

Section 2

A group of people has just arrived at their hotel for a two-week holiday. The hotel manager is talking to them about some hotel facilities and rules. First, you have some time to look at questions 11 to 17.

Now listen and answer questions 11 to 17.

Welcome, everyone, it's nice to see all of you here. I'd like to tell you a bit about the hotel, including a few 'dos' and 'don'ts'. I know you've just had a long trip, so I'll keep it brief so that you can go to your rooms and put your feet up.

We want you to relax and enjoy the casual atmosphere of this place – you *are* on holidays, after all – but I'd ask you not to walk around in bare feet, it's just that it's so easy to bring sand into the building when you come back from the beach, so we'd appreciate it if you could at least <u>wear shoes while on the premises</u>. Oh, and if you want to hire some equipment, you'll find a good range of gear such as beach umbrellas, surfboards and snorkelling equipment down at the <u>beach cafe</u> for quite reasonable rates. We used to hire out such things from reception, but that was discontinued last year.

If you do need to speak to someone at reception, there are staff on duty there seven days a week, usually either myself, Maureen or Bruce. The early risers among you might like to go down to the beach to see the sun rise at 6 o'clock, but we're <u>not open till seven in the morning and we're here until six in the evening</u>. You'll also find a range of brochures about activities and attractions in the district. If you need to contact hotel staff after hours, you can just call 7946 from the phone in your room. The cleaners come in to vacuum the rooms and clean the bathrooms every second day, and the bed sheets and towels are changed <u>twice a week, on Tuesdays and Fridays</u>.

Smoking is not allowed inside the building and we'd also ask you to refrain from smoking when you're near the swimming pool area. If you do need to have a cigarette, you can go out <u>onto your balcony</u>, where you'll also find an ashtray. When you're sitting out on your balcony, you might get a visit from some of the local <u>birds</u>. They're very colourful and friendly, but we'd ask you to resist the temptation to give them something to eat because they can quickly become dependent on handouts. There's a pond in the garden at the back of the hotel and we'd appreciate it if you didn't feed the <u>fish</u> – they can get quite ill unless they're given the right kind of food. Just one point on noise – there's a general house rule to keep noise to a minimum <u>after 11 at night</u>. It's fine to enjoy music and lively conversation, but it's important to be considerate and respect everyone's right to have a good sleep.

You now have some time to look at questions 18 to 20.

Now listen and answer questions 18 to 20.

I didn't mean to take up so much of your time, but I've just remembered that I need to tell you a few things about the disposal of garbage. We do like to do things in an environmentally friendly manner around here, and so we recycle garbage where possible. There are separate bins for glass and metal but we don't yet have a facility in this area for the recycling of <u>plastic</u>, so that should just go in with your general unrecyclable waste along with <u>food scraps</u>. The gardener wishes he could use them to make compost for the garden, but that's a little impractical at present. It'd be good if you could leave your old newspapers at reception – the local school is involved in a recycling project and they send someone to the hotel to pick them up.

If it's raining and you don't feel like going out, there are plenty of ways to pass the time in the hotel. There's a gym on the second floor if you want to get some exercise and a couple of billiard tables in a room next to the gym. For relaxation, there's a <u>coin-operated spa</u>, which is also located on the second floor. If you'd like to watch a movie, you can borrow a DVD from reception and watch it in your room. Also, if you've brought your laptop with you, you can <u>connect to the Internet in your room for a small fee</u>.

All these rules are designed to ensure you have a pleasant stay here. If any of you has the energy to go out tonight, you'll find there's plenty to do. Just around the corner there's a <u>nightclub</u> if you feel like some dancing, but if you want to have a few drinks without the music, there's a bar in the centre of town, but you'll need to take a taxi to get there. There's also a cinema and even a casino down there. If you like to sing, you'll find a <u>karaoke club</u> right across the road from the hotel. Anyway, I hope you all have a very happy stay with us.

That is the end of Section 2. You now have half a minute to check your answers.

Now turn to Section 3.

Section 3

You will hear a discussion between a nursing student and a tutor after the student has done some practical training at a home nursing service for older patients. First, you will have some time to look at questions 21 to 26.

Now listen and answer questions 21 to 26.

Tutor: Now, you spent last week doing practical training with the home nursing service dealing with elderly patients. How did it go?

Student: Oh, it was pretty good. I mean, I learnt a lot since I hadn't had much to do with older patients before.

Tutor: Well, with our ageing population, care of the elderly is a major focus of the healthcare system, and quite a range of healthcare professionals are called upon.

Student: Yes, I was surprised in a few cases. For instance, we know that preventing falls is very important. There's a separate falls clinic, but if a patient appears to be <u>unsteady on their feet</u>, whether they're walking unaided or using a walking stick or a frame, the nurse has to get in touch with a <u>physiotherapist</u>.

Tutor: That's right. We always need to be on the lookout for signs of deteriorating health. If you notice that a patient is <u>becoming disoriented</u>, it could be caused by tiredness or the side effects of medication. So what you have to do is contact their <u>doctor</u>, who will then assess what the cause could be.

Student: Yeah. Sometimes it's hard to work out exactly what's wrong. There was one patient who bumped into furniture a few times in her own living room while we were there.

Tutor: Well, as you know, our <u>vision can deteriorate</u> with age, and in the case of elderly patients, we need to refer them to an <u>occupational therapist</u> if they're experiencing problems due to visual impairment. If necessary, it's up to that specialist to refer them to an optometrist.

Student: I see. What about the patients who don't want our help? I mean, they're free to live their lives as they want and we can't force them to see a doctor or someone.

Tutor: Yes, it's not unusual for our patients to <u>decline assistance</u>, especially the men. It's often a matter of pride or an overestimation of their own capabilities. But when there are potentially serious issues that could have a long-term impact on their health and safety, we get the <u>aged care team</u> to pay them a visit. Sometimes they just end up having a friendly chat, but at least they're informed about what services are available.

Student: So they provide a bit of psychological help, like a doctor often does. What about when a patient appears to be becoming increasingly <u>frail</u>? I mean, there could be a whole number of causes like the time of day or just simply old age.

Tutor: You need to remember that sometimes elderly patients can't go shopping regularly, or they can't afford much nutritious food. Because it can be a mixture of reasons that might need to be addressed by their doctor or the aged care team, we first contact a <u>dietician</u> because we find that almost everyone can benefit from an expert review of the types of food they're eating.

Student: What about the patients who have pets? I mean, I've been into some people's homes and they seem to be a kind of health hazard, especially the ones with a lot of cats, or birds in cages.

Tutor: Well, <u>pets</u> do a lot of good for humans – they provide company, they're a reason to get some exercise, particularly dogs, and generally they do more good than harm. But you're right, they can spread disease and also dogs and cats can trip up their owners. We used to let the occupational therapist handle that issue, but now if we have concerns, we give the <u>falls clinic</u> a call for a home assessment.

Student: Oh right, I'll just make a note about that.

Before you hear the rest of the conversation, you have some time to look at questions 27 to 30.

Now listen and answer questions 27 to 30.

Student: Some of the patients we visited last week had dementia, so I'd just like to clarify a few things about that if you don't mind.

Tutor: No, that's fine. With increasing life expectancy we're going to be seeing more and more of it.

Student: I know that dementia can be caused by genetic or environmental factors, such as over-indulging in alcohol over a long period of time, but it seems that it can be difficult to diagnose dementia because its symptoms can occur with various other conditions.

Tutor: That's right. Some of them, such as Pick's disease, can't be overcome, whereas others, such as <u>brain tumours, can</u>.

Student: One of the patients we saw appeared to be very <u>anxious</u>. I thought that might've been a side effect of the medication she was on, but the nurse I was training with told me it was a frequently occurring syndrome of people with dementia. They're <u>upset at not being able to do some of the things they could in the past and often don't trust those around them</u>.

Tutor: And many healthy people get anxious about the future, whether it's about things going on in their own lives or what's happening in the wider world. It's good though – one of life's pleasures that people with dementia continue to enjoy is food. Generally we find they're keen on cakes and desserts, so you have to make sure they have a balanced diet overall. Elderly people with dentures may avoid chewy food, and their taste receptors for salt can become diminished, which is a normal part of ageing.

Student: We had some lectures last month about research done on therapies to enhance the well-being of all kinds of age groups. For example, they told us that children recovering from surgery really like to sing if they've got the energy, people with dementia usually experience a lift in their mood while listening to music, and people with depression nearly always benefit from doing regular exercise.

Tutor: Yes, it's very rewarding to see patients responding to measures like those and it helps us view their health from a broader perspective.

That is the end of Section 3. You now have half a minute to check your answers.

Now turn to Section 4.

Section 4

You will hear a lecture to anthropology students about an ethnic group called the Tuareg. Many of these people live in the Sahara desert in Africa. First, you have some time to look at questions 31 to 40.

Now listen and answer questions 31 to 40.

Good afternoon, everyone. In today's lecture I'll be outlining some of the main economic activities of the Tuareg. The Tuareg are an ethnic group who live in north and west Africa, mostly in the Sahara desert and surrounding regions. There is no consensus on the size of the Tuareg population today, with most estimates ranging between 750,000 and 1.3 million people. The main reason for this uncertainty is their nomadic lifestyle; it's always difficult to conduct a census among people who do not live in permanent settlements. The Sahara is known around the world as a very arid region, and the ability of these people to survive in such an inhospitable environment is amazing. The Tuareg have sometimes been referred to as 'the blue people' because the indigo dye that is used to colour their clothing often comes off on their skin, giving it a blue colouring. Their staple diet consists of millet, a grain that they use to make porridge, as well as rice, wheat and other grains. In the dry season their staple foods are grain and dates, whereas in the cooler, wet season they have more milk and meat.

These days most Tuareg living in rural areas pursue a range of activities. These include the herding and breeding of livestock, carrying out gardening in the oases, and of course trade, which they have conducted for millennia. For more than 2,000 years they have operated camel caravans – these are groups of camels that carry goods over long distances, trading products between the Sahel region south of the Sahara up to the Mediterranean Sea on the coast of north Africa. The camel caravans, sometimes consisting of more than 20,000 camels, dominated trans-Saharan trade until the middle of the 20th century. A strong camel can carry up to a total of 300 kilograms of goods, excluding the rider. These caravans often cross the Sahara to the Sahel region to the south. At first the pace is slow to allow the camels to feed, but as they enter the barren desert where there is nothing to eat, they walk from morning to night, typically covering 50 kilometres in a day. In the semi-arid Sahel region, which receives between 10 and 50 centimetres of rainfall per year, the Tuareg obtain cloth as well as millet grown by the Hausa people. In exchange for these, the Tuareg give them a number of products, in particular salt and dates. Although camels are still used, these days goods are more often carried by truck and train.

The Tuareg also grow some of their own food. Crops grown by the Tuareg include millet, barley, wheat, maize, onions, tomatoes and dates. In farming, there is a division of labour based on gender, with the men planting and irrigating the gardens, and the women harvesting the crops. Herding animals is also an important economic activity. The livestock Tuareg particularly value are camels and cattle rather than the smaller animals such as goats. In regard to herding animals, men usually take care of the camels, while the women look after the goats, sheep and donkeys.

For more than 1,000 years the Tuareg have been involved in the salt trade. The salt is obtained by digging pits 6 to 8 metres deep to reach water with a very high salt content, also known as brine. The summer heat evaporates the water, leaving the salt behind. The salt is then formed into blocks, which weigh around 21 kilograms, and packed into the hollowed-out trunks of palm trees. These are then wrapped in straw and loaded onto camels to be traded elsewhere. The price of salt rises with the approach of summer because this is the time of year when animals need it most. The best quality salt is used for human consumption, and the lower quality salt is given to animals.

One group among the Tuareg that is not involved in the camel caravans and farming are the craftsmen who make the distinctive jewellery and handicrafts. Traditionally they had lower status due to their more sedentary lifestyle – the Tuareg have always prized and enjoyed the freedom of a nomadic way of life, whereas the craftsmen need to stay in one place with their tools and workshops. However, for this same reason they were always able to gain a higher level of education than other Tuareg groups. With gradual modernisation, their higher education levels have come to be of more benefit to them, in addition to which their jewellery and leather goods have found a market among visitors from abroad.

The economic power of the Tuareg has deteriorated since countries in the region gained their independence in the 1960s and under the impact of severe droughts. Though most Tuareg continue to live as nomads, their traditional way of life is undergoing significant change.

That is the end of Section 4. You now have half a minute to check your answers.

That is the end of the Listening Test. You now have ten minutes to transfer your answers to the answer sheet.

Listening Test 2

You will hear four different recordings and you will have to answer questions on what you hear.

There will be time for you to read the instructions and questions before the recording is played.

You will also have the opportunity to check your answers.

The recordings will be played ONCE only.

The test is in four sections. Write your answers on the question sheet as you listen. At the end of Section 4, you have ten minutes to transfer your answers onto the answer sheet, which is on page 31. When you finish, check the answers at the back of the book.

Now turn to Section 1.

Section 1

You will hear a woman who is applying for a driving licence. First, you have some time to look at questions 1 to 5.

Now listen and answer questions 1 to 5.

Man: Good morning, can I help you?

Woman: I'd like to apply for a driving licence.

Man: Right. We'll just have to fill in this form.

Woman: Uh-huh.

Man: First, er, could you tell me your full name?

Woman: Yes, it's Theresa Collins.

Man: Right.

The woman says her name is Theresa Collins, so 'Theresa Collins' has been written next to the example on the question paper. Now continue with questions 1 to 5.

Man: And what type of vehicle would you like to drive?

Woman: Oh, just a normal car.

Man: That's a Class C licence then. And have you ever held a driving licence in another country?

Woman: Oh no, I'm too young. Anyway, I think I'd be too scared to drive in another country.

Man: Right. I'll just need to get some personal details from you. Um, could I have your date of birth, please?

Woman: Yes, it's the 17th of March 1994.

Man: And what's your address?

Woman: 28 River Street.

Man: That's spelt R-i-v-e-r, is that right?

Woman: Yes.

Man: And that's in Bentley, isn't it?

Woman: Yes.

Man: OK. And your phone number?

Woman: I'll give you my home number. It's 3701 8699.

Man: Right. And what form of ID do you have with you?

Woman: Well, I've got a bank card. Here it is.

Man: Let's see. No, we need something with your photo on it, like a student card.

Woman: I've got that with me, here you are.

Man: Yeah, that's fine. Now, there's an application fee of $55. How would you like to pay? We take credit cards but not cheques, I'm afraid. And we take cash of course, if you have enough money with you.

Woman: I do actually, and I try not to use my credit card if I can avoid it. Here you are.

Man: Thank you.

Before you hear the rest of the conversation, you have some time to look at questions 6 to 10.

Now listen and answer questions 6 to 10.

Man: Right, now there are a few things I need to tell you about the licence. Before you actually drive a car, you have to pass a test about the road rules.

Woman: Oh, that's the test about speed limits and road signs and things like that, isn't it?

Man: Yes, that's right. There are two parts to the test, and you're allowed to make a maximum of two errors in each section, so that's four altogether.

Woman: And if I fail the test, can I do it again?

Man: Yes you can, but you have to wait at least a week.

Woman: Right. And when I'm driving, there's got to be someone with me in the car who holds a full licence, doesn't there?

Man: Yes. That could be a family member, a professional driving instructor or a friend.

Woman: What about my older sister?

Man: Sure, as long as she's got the right kind of licence. Now the learner's licence is valid for nine months. At the end of that time you have to do a practical driving test. If you pass that, you're granted a provisional licence. That expires after 18 months. If you don't pass the practical driving test, you are given a learner's licence for another six months.

Woman: I see. And while I'm still on the learner's licence, how fast can I drive?

Man: Well, it depends on the area you're driving in. In most places in the city, there's a speed limit of 60 kilometres an hour. As you probably know, on highways in the countryside there's often a speed limit of 100 kilometres per hour. But as a learner you're never allowed to exceed 80, even on a highway.

Woman: Right. I think that'd be fast enough for me anyway.

Man: Is there anything else you need to know?

Woman: Oh yeah, I heard there are restrictions on using mobile phones while you're driving.

Man: That's right. Until recently, you could only talk on a mobile while you're driving if you used an earphone or hands-free device, but that's been changed.

Woman: Oh?

Man: Yeah. Now you can't use mobiles at all while driving.

Woman: Not even to send an SMS?

Man: Not even to send an SMS. Anyway, if that's all, I'll give you a copy of the book on the road rules.

Woman: Thanks very much.

This is the end of Section 1. You now have half a minute to check your answers.

Now turn to Section 2.

Section 2

You will hear a training officer giving a talk to new staff who will be working at the information desk at an airport. First, you have some time to look at questions 11 to 15.

Now listen and answer questions 11 to 15.

Now, when you're working at the information desk in the arrivals section of the airport, one of the most common questions people ask is, what's the best way to get to their hotel or to a particular address once they leave the airport. The answer you give them depends on a number of factors, so I'm going to give you a few general tips to help you deal with these issues by taking the case of a typical destination for the average traveller.

After a long flight, people are often tired and want to get to their final destination as soon as possible. You'd think that the quickest way would be to take a taxi, but because of traffic congestion, it turns out that it's usually better to take the train. Trains are cheaper than taxis, and taxis get caught in traffic jams and they can't go through red lights. For some passengers, the most important consideration is to take a means of transport that is going to run according to schedule. Now, you would think that the train would be the best one for this, but as the airport train is operated by a private company, there have been a lot of problems integrating its running times with the publicly owned train network, and this has resulted in a lot of delays. Surveys on travelling to and from the airport have found that minibuses are the most dependable form of transport.

There are other considerations too. If a person wants a comfortable ride with plenty of legroom after a long flight in a cramped seat, it'd be best for them to take one of the large, air-conditioned buses. It's a new fleet with plenty of space for luggage and, on top of that, they're much cheaper than taxis. Some passengers are far more concerned about security; of course we can't guarantee that they won't be robbed or even cheated by a dishonest driver, so I think for them the best thing to do is to get someone who they know and trust to pick them up in their car. Finally, there's also the 'green' traveller who wants to cause the least possible pollution. Now, obviously we can't tell them to walk because it's too far, particularly with heavy luggage. You might guess that public transport would be the cleanest way to travel, but it turns out that it's taxis, and that's because of the type of fuel they use. They're also not surprisingly the most popular choice of businesspeople.

You now have 30 seconds to look at questions 16 to 20.

Now listen and answer questions 16 to 20.

So far we've been focusing on the arrivals section of the airport. Now we're going to be looking at the departures section. You've all got a copy of the floor plan of the departures section of the airport. Because of the recent renovations, a lot of people are disoriented when they see it for the first time, so you need to be familiar with the new layout. At the bottom of the floor plan you can see where the passengers check in. They then go through security control and in front of them is the information desk, right in the middle of the whole floor plan. Just to the right of the information desk there's a newsagency where you can buy newspapers and magazines. For those who like to do a bit of shopping, to the left of the information desk we have a jewellery

store – it's well worth a look at – and a well-stocked electronics goods shop, and between those two there is a pharmacy. There used to be a dress shop in that position. At the top right-hand corner of the diagram we have the waiting lounge and the exit to the planes.

In the top left-hand corner are the public toilets. You can use those toilets or, if you like, there are also staff facilities near the bookshop, but you'll need to get the key. Just behind the information desk we have some food outlets and over to the right, next to the waiting lounge, is a cafe. When the renovations are completed it will function as an Internet cafe. At most airports you get people congregating on the footpath smoking, which is unpleasant for the non-smokers entering and leaving the building. For that reason we've set up a dedicated smoking room inside the terminal, next to the bookshop. It's well ventilated and looks out onto the tarmac. The original plan was to put a wine bar next to the bookshop, but there were problems with the licensing laws.

I'd encourage you to walk around the airport to familiarise yourselves with the layout so that you can more easily handle passengers' enquiries.

That is the end of Section 2. You now have half a minute to check your answers.

Now turn to Section 3.

Section 3

You will hear two college students reporting to their science class about a project they have done on an Australian animal called the Tasmanian devil. First, you have some time to look at questions 21 to 26.

Now listen and answer questions 21 to 26.

Woman: Hi, everyone. For our assignment on a native animal, George and I chose that unusual Australian creature, the Tasmanian devil.

Man: Yeah. Actually, they don't deserve to be called 'devils', though they do have some strange habits.

Woman: Anyway, as their name indicates, they're only found in the wild on the island of Tasmania. You can find them all over the island, including in the south-west rainforests and in coastal heath areas, but they're most commonly found in the forests where there's less rainfall, in the eastern and northern parts of the island.

Man: In fact, they live any place where they can get shelter during the day and food at night.

Woman: Some of you may have seen one in a zoo. They're about the size of a small dog and are covered with short, soft, black fur with white markings on some parts of their bodies. An adult male can weigh from 5 to 13 kilograms, and a female from 4.5 to 9 kilograms.

Man: They've got a large head and neck, with heavy limbs. They're called devils because of the terrible sounds they make at night. This has given them an undeserved reputation for being aggressive, whereas in fact they're fairly shy creatures, but this doesn't mean that they're tame or friendly enough to be pets.

Woman: And like kangaroos, they carry their young in a pouch. They have babies only once a year, and then about 20 are born at one time, but at that stage they're only as big as a grain of rice. The babies have a race to the pouch, because there are only four teats there, and the mothers rear an average of three young annually.

Man: The babies stay in the pouch for about five months. Then they're left in their nest or are carried on their mother's back when she goes out, and eventually they have to look after themselves at about eight months. Then they in turn start breeding at the end of their second year.

Woman: And around 60% of them die in their first summer due to the tough competition for food. The ones that survive can live for up to seven years, which means they don't live as long as the average domestic dog.

Man: No. And it's estimated that now there are between 100,000 and 150,000 of them altogether. They were almost wiped out by the early European settlers because they hated the devils eating their chickens, so the government paid people to kill Tasmanian devils.

Woman: And most farmers still dislike them. Their numbers fell so drastically due to farmers poisoning them or shooting them that it was thought that they might have become extinct. Then a law was passed in 1941 to protect them, and since then their numbers have grown again.

Before you hear the rest of the talk, you have some time to look at questions 27 to 30.

Now listen and answer questions 27 to 30.

Man: Now we'd like to talk about some of their habits. They live alone in places such as hollow logs, caves or in burrows underground, which they line with bark, grass and leaves. They usually move slowly and look clumsy when they move quickly, but the young ones are more agile and can even climb trees.

Woman: But one of the most amazing things about Tasmanian devils is how and what they eat. They've got incredibly strong teeth and jaws, so a large male can give you a bite as strong as a 50-kilogram dog!

Man: But don't worry, they don't eat people! Some farmers complain about them taking young lambs, but their diet consists predominantly of animals that have already died. They don't get ill when they eat sick animals because of the digestive enzymes in their own stomachs that kill the diseases.

Woman: And they've got an undeserved reputation for being smelly, whereas in fact they wash themselves as much as cats do. They're nocturnal animals, so they go hunting at night, often travelling up to 15 kilometres and using their strong sense of smell to find food. They eat all kinds of animals – and they eat everything, including fur, and leave nothing behind except the largest bones.

Man: Yeah, there can be up to 22 of them feeding off one carcass at the same time, and they're very greedy, noisy eaters. In all the excitement of eating, there's a lot of coughing, barking and so on. It's quite common for them to bite each other to decide who can eat first, who goes second and so on.

Woman: And they've got an incredible appetite. They can eat the equivalent of 40% of their own body weight in just half an hour, which is like a human eating about 25 kilograms of steak. And they make really good use of their strong, blunt teeth. When they're frightened, they show them by yawning, which is more effective than biting or barking.

Man: But the only serious fighting that takes place is when they're looking for a mate. All in all, they're a fascinating little animal.

That is the end of Section 3. You now have half a minute to check your answers.

Now turn to Section 4.

Section 4

You will hear a lecture by a healthcare researcher to students of health science about the results of a survey on yoga in Australia. First, you have some time to look at questions 31 to 40.

Now listen and answer questions 31 to 40.

Good afternoon everyone. In today's lecture I'm going to present some of the findings of the largest and most comprehensive survey of yoga practice ever conducted in Australia. The objectives of this survey were to investigate the characteristics of people who practise yoga in this country, ah the styles and techniques of yoga that are practised, how often people practise yoga, the reasons why they do yoga and the perceived benefits of yoga practice. It is our hope that the findings of this survey will be of help to both teachers and students of yoga in this country and abroad, as well as to healthcare practitioners. Prior to our study, no nationwide research had been conducted into the topic. Our research team decided to do a web-based survey so that we would reach the maximum possible number of people all around the country, and also due to our funding limitations. The survey was promoted through yoga schools, the media and by word of mouth. Eventually, ah almost 4,000 people responded to the survey, which took about 30 minutes to complete. About one-third of the people who filled in the survey were yoga teachers, the other two-thirds were yoga students; overall, 85% of the respondents were women.

Yoga means different things to different people and, reflecting its diversity, there are many types of yoga. Our survey found that it is males and younger people who are more attracted to some of the physically more demanding styles of yoga that have gained in popularity in the West over the past two decades, whereas older age groups went for more relaxing styles. Apart from providing exercise, yoga can also be a form of therapy, meditation or a spiritual path.

Government agencies have found that around 2% of the adult population practise yoga to a greater or lesser extent, with a much lower participation rate for people who have not yet turned 18. Both their research and our survey found that the age group with the highest participation rate in yoga classes is the 35- to 44-year-old group. There has been a slight decline recently in the popularity of yoga; however, this was in the context of a reduction in physical activities overall among the Australian population. A major reason for this trend is not the rise in the popularity of junk food but because more and more people are playing computer games.

56% of the yoga students who responded to our survey attend class once or twice a week. In contrast, and not surprisingly, the same percentage of the yoga teachers in our survey said they taught or practised yoga between five and seven times per week. Most people initially take up yoga to improve their health and fitness – with an emphasis on flexibility and strength – but also in order to reduce stress or as a treatment for a physical problem, particularly for a bad back. Many of the respondents to our survey stated that their reasons for doing yoga changed after they started doing regular practice, with more than half claiming that they keep at it for their personal development, which could be interpreted in a variety of ways.

Although overall yoga promotes physical and mental health, it can cause damage if not done properly, and care needs to be taken with inverted postures such as the headstand and shoulder stand, as well as with the lotus position, which is the cross-legged position that is commonly associated with yoga and meditation. A common admission in the survey among those who had sustained injuries was that they had pushed themselves too hard. Far less frequently teachers were said to have caused injuries by pushing students too hard.

A large number of our survey respondents reported that they work in health care occupations, and for most of the yoga teachers, teaching yoga is not their only source of income. Among the students the most common health care occupation is nursing, whereas among teachers the largest group worked as massage therapists. Many also worked as nurses, psychologists and practitioners of alternative medicine.

In the survey we also looked at incomes. We didn't ask for individual incomes, but household incomes; that is, the total income of all the people that survey respondents lived with. We found that around three-quarters of the students and 60% of the teachers have a household income above $50,000 per year. Whereas just 9% of the students are on an annual household income below $30,000, one in five of the teachers belong to this group. It would seem that being a yoga teacher is not a path to riches. Yoga itself isn't that expensive, with the average person spending just under $100 a month on yoga practice and accessories.

Overall, yoga was found to have a positive impact on people's lives, with a clear majority concluding that their physical, mental and emotional health, as well as their relationships, were better or much better than before they started doing yoga.

That is the end of Section 4. You now have half a minute to check your answers.

That is the end of the Listening Test. You now have ten minutes to transfer your answers to the answer sheet.

Listening Test 3

You will hear four different recordings and you will have to answer questions on what you hear.

There will be time for you to read the instructions and questions before the recording is played.

You will also have the opportunity to check your answers.

The recordings will be played ONCE only.

The test is in four sections. Write your answers on the question sheet as you listen. At the end of Section 4, you have ten minutes to transfer your answers onto the answer sheet, which is on page 31. When you finish, check the answers at the back of the book.

Now turn to Section 1.

Section 1

You will hear a man having an interview for a job in a hotel. First, you have some time to look at questions 1 to 4.

Now listen and answer questions 1 to 4.

Woman: Good morning, Mr Peters, please come in and have a seat.

Man: Thank you.

Woman: My name's Gloria McKell, I'm the personnel manager here. Now, before we start the job interview, I just need to get a couple of details from you.

Man: Sure.

Woman: Now, first of all I'd just like to confirm I have the correct details. Your name is George Peters, isn't it?

Man: Yes.

Woman: And your contact phone number is 0438 637 935?

Man: That's right.

The man's phone number is 0438 637 935, so '0438 637 935' has been written next to the example on the question paper. Now continue with questions 1 to 4.

Woman: We have vacancies for a couple of positions in our hotel at the moment. Uh, which position are you interested in applying for?

Man: Uh, room service.

Woman: Room service, right. Now I'd like to find out a little about your employment background. Have you worked in a hotel before, or have you been employed in any capacity in the hospitality industry?

Man: I've never actually worked in a hotel, but I've been a waiter in a couple of different places.

Woman: Oh, good. I'm sure that experience will come in handy.

Man: Also, at the moment I'm doing a course.

Woman: Oh, what are you doing?

Man: I'm studying Tourism Management. I'm in the second year of a three-year course.

Woman: That's good to hear. Oh, by the way, we have quite a few international guests staying here. Do you speak any foreign languages?

Man: I did French at high school, and I'm studying Korean as part of my diploma course.

Woman: And how well do you speak those languages?

Man: Well, I can have a simple conversation in French, but my Korean's still fairly basic, though I think it'd come in handy with room service.

Woman: Good.

Before you hear the rest of the conversation, you have some time to look at questions 5 to 10.

Now listen and answer questions 5 to 10.

Woman: Well, I've asked you a number of questions, now I wonder if there's anything you'd like to know about the position or about the hotel.

Man: Um, could you tell me what the duties are of doing room service? I mean, I've got a vague idea, but it'd be good to know exactly what it involves.

Woman: Yes, of course. In fact, your duties would not be limited to room service; there are a few extra things that are now part of the job you're applying for. For instance, the porter used to <u>carry guests' bags to their rooms</u>, but his position has been abolished and that would now be your responsibility. Unlike a waiter, you don't take their orders for food – the kitchen staff does that by phone.

Man: Right.

Woman: If you're on afternoon shift, you also have to take the afternoon newspapers to the guests who've ordered them, but if you're on the morning shift it's done by the concierge. You're qualified to serve alcohol, aren't you?

Man: Yes.

Woman: Good, because on evening shifts you may have to <u>serve in the hotel bar</u>. What else? If a guest calls to say there's a problem with some of the equipment in the room, if it's something simple like one of the light bulbs has blown, then you replace it, but if it's something more complex, say, if the TV isn't working, you leave that to the technical staff.

Man: I see.

Woman: Oh no, sorry, there's been a change in that. In fact, now all electrical work has to be done by the technical staff – it's an occupational health and safety issue.

Man: Better to be safe than sorry, I suppose.

Woman: Yes. You don't have to do any of the cleaning, though you do have to <u>remove any dirty plates the guests have used in their rooms</u>. The cleaners are the ones who make sure the fridges have the right amount of drinks and snacks in them. There are a few other duties, but basically room service plays an important role in maintaining guest satisfaction, and so a friendly attitude and efficiency are what's required.

Man: Oh, that goes without saying. And could I ask about the pay and conditions?

Woman: Of course. The pay's $20 per hour, and $25 per hour between 10 pm and 6 am as well as on Sundays.

Man: Right. And what's provided by the hotel? For instance, I suppose there's a uniform to wear?

Woman: Yes, <u>the hotel provides the jacket and trousers</u>. However, you'd be responsible for doing your own laundry.

Man: Uh-huh. Oh yeah, um, what about transport? Like, if we finish a shift around midnight, does the hotel pay for taxi fares to get back home?

Woman: We used to do that, but now instead <u>we allow staff to park for free</u> on the premises. It can be very hard finding a parking space on the street around this area.

Man: Yeah, I had trouble getting a spot when I came here today.

Woman: Yes, it's a busy area. I might just add that we pride ourselves on having a well-trained staff, so it's a good thing that you're doing your diploma.

Man: Yes, it's been a very interesting course so far.

Woman: Good. Oh, one other thing, <u>we also pay for medical insurance</u> for all our employees as an extra incentive for working with us.

Man: Oh, that's good.

Woman: And until recently we provided one meal per shift as well, but that's been discontinued. Right, well I think that's all then. I'll give you a call later in the week and we can talk further.

Man: Uh-huh. Well, thank you very much.

That is the end of Section 1. You now have half a minute to check your answers.

Now turn to Section 2.

Section 2

Timothy Curtin is an officer at the Department of Immigration. You will hear him talking to foreign students at a business college regarding visa regulations. First, you have some time to look at questions 11 and 12.

Now listen and answer questions 11 to 12.

Good morning, everyone. My name's Timothy Curtin, and I work for the Department of Immigration. I've come along today to give you some information about visa regulations so as to make your stay here a bit easier. I'll be telling you about some of the rules for those on student visas and particularly about how to extend your visa.

Now, I'm from the Atwood office of the Department of Immigration. At our office we mainly <u>process work visas</u>. However, in the office where I used to work, I dealt mainly with <u>student visas</u>, which is why I was chosen to speak to you today. For other matters such as residency applications or medical visas, you need to go to the Hampstead office of the department. For <u>visas for people who are here on holidays</u> you can go to any office of the Department of Immigration.

As you would know, there are certain conditions for people who hold student visas. For instance, if you move, you have to tell your college. The college then has to inform the department by mail, giving both your old and new address. You can change the college where you study, but <u>you have to let the department know that you've enrolled with a new college</u>. You're also allowed to work, but remember that the maximum you can work is 15 hours per week because you're here as full-time students, so your main focus has to be on studies. You can also take up to three weeks' holidays between courses. <u>If your marital status changes, you have to inform the department</u> and provide us with a copy of the marriage certificate within a month of the wedding.

Before you hear the rest of the talk, you have some time to look at questions 13 to 20.

Now listen and answer questions 13 to 20.

What I'd like to do now is to go through the steps you have to follow when you want to extend your student visa, because a lot of students have to do that at some point while they're in this country.

The first thing you have to do if you want to extend your visa is to pay for the next course you're planning to take. As you know, all courses have to be paid in advance. The course itself has to be of at least <u>four months' duration</u> and you are advised to submit your visa application at least two months before the course is due to commence, if possible. You need to keep a copy of the receipt of payment and send us the original. We advise that with all the documents you send us that you keep photocopies for yourself just in case any go missing. You'll also have to get a letter from the college you've been attending, which states your attendance record at that college. You already know that one of the requirements of a student visa is that you turn up to a minimum of 75% of your classes. If you've been absent from more than 25% of classes, you'll have to provide medical certificates stating that you were ill and unable to attend classes on those days.

You then need to fill in a form to extend your student visa. That's Form 726C. You can obtain one by visiting any branch of our department, or else you can access it on the Internet. At the end of my talk I'll be handing out a brochure that gives our website address as well as the addresses of department offices throughout the country. On top of that, you'll also need to be able to show that you have the means to support yourself while in this country. It's been estimated that the average student needs $15,000 a year to live on, and for that reason you will need to prove that you've got at least $6,000 in a bank account. It's got to be a bank account in this country, so $10,000 in a foreign account is of no use. Of course, your passport has to be still valid. And what else? Ah yes, then you'll need three passport photos. Make sure they're fairly recent photos. You then take all these documents and the form down to the Immigration office, along with your passport. As you can see, there's quite a lot to do, so don't leave it till the last minute.

You've got to lodge your application, along with all the documents, at least three weeks before the old visa expires. You have to pay for the visa application too, and that money's non-refundable. You can pay by cash, credit card or cheque. Oh, by the way, it'll cost you $325 to apply for an extension of your student visa. Wait, let me check that. Oh, that's right, it's gone up to $435. Then, it'll take about a week to process your application, but we also have to make allowances for weekends and public holidays, and at times we have heavy workloads, so it may take as long as 12 working days before you get a reply. You might hear from us before that, but don't contact us before that period of time has passed. There may be a few things we need to ask you about before granting a visa, so there's a chance you'll be invited to an interview just so that we can check up on anything. But we'll let you know if we think that's necessary.

Don't worry if you can't remember all these things I've been talking about, they're all on Form 726C. Well, I think that's about enough from me. Now, do any of you have any questions?

That is the end of Section 2. You now have half a minute to check your answers.

Now turn to Section 3.

Section 3

You will hear two marketing students, Maggie and Mike, talking to their teacher about a seminar presentation that they are preparing. First, you have some time to look at questions 21 to 24.

Now listen and answer questions 21 to 24.

Teacher: So, you two are going to give a presentation next week about the beauty industry, aren't you?

Mike: Yeah, we've divided it into two sections. First we'll be looking at the place of the beauty industry in the economy.

Maggie: Yeah, and then we were going to look at what drives it, as well as some recent trends.

Teacher: That sounds like a good way of doing it. OK, Mike, how are you going to be starting off?

Mike: Well, first we were amazed at the size of the industry. It's measured in billions, not millions. It's worth $160 billion a year globally.

Maggie: That figure includes products for haircare – they're worth $38 billion alone. Then there's make-up and perfume – I think that's $15 billion – plus cosmetic surgery, skincare products, diet pills and health clubs.

Mike: In America, more money is spent on beauty than on education.

Teacher: Really?

Maggie: Yeah. The profits of the leading company in the industry have been growing by 14% a year for the last 13 years. And the industry as a whole has been growing at the rate of 7% a year. In India, sales of anti-ageing creams are growing by 40% a year. And you know the Avon ladies? Well, there are 900,000 of them in Brazil, which is more than the number of people in its navy and army.

Teacher: Amazing. Now, just going back a bit, you mentioned cosmetic surgery. Do you have any data on that?

Mike: Yeah. It's worth $20 billion a year now, and the number of procedures they do in the US has jumped by more than 220% since 1997. Botox injections to remove wrinkles are the main thing done these days, but nose jobs and fat removal are still very common. And there's been a real boom in teeth whitening. Also, because the cost of cosmetic surgery has really come down, a lot more people can afford it now.

Teacher: And do you know much about the history of the industry?

Maggie: Well, the modern beauty industry really started up about a hundred years ago. When photography became widespread, it became much easier for the public to see idealised standards of beauty, and people wanted to buy the products to make themselves look like the models they saw in magazines. By the middle of the century, scientific advances led to changes in the ingredients used in many cosmetics, which made them more affordable, and packaging made them more attractive.

Before you hear the rest of the conversation, you have some time to look at questions 25 to 30.

Now listen and answer questions 25 to 30.

Teacher: Now, in the second part of your presentation you're going to be looking at why people buy the products.

Maggie: Yes, that's right. This area is a bit more subjective, and Mike and I disagreed on a few matters.

Mike: Well, marketing is a hit-and-miss affair and it's true what they say, that only half of any marketing budget achieves the desired result.

Maggie: I think that's an exaggeration, don't you? Anyway, there are powerful forces at work in the beauty industry, because when it comes down to it, there's no avoiding the fact that it's all about image and that this industry is so successful because it preys on people's hopes and fears.

Mike: That's a bit harsh, isn't it? It's only natural to try to look your best.

Maggie: Well, the guy who founded Revlon called the whole business 'hope in a jar'.

Teacher: Did he? That's a nice way of putting it.

Mike: We found a British study of 11,000 people which concluded that people who are less attractive earn less money.

Maggie: And that was the case no matter whether they worked as secretaries, in sales or as executives.

Teacher: And why do you think that's the case?

Maggie: Well, I reckon one reason is because attractive people have higher expectations and are less willing to put up with being treated badly.

Mike: Yeah, but there are plenty of good-looking people with low self-esteem who *do* let others walk all over them. I think what it comes down to is that people in general treat good-looking people well. And it starts young. Even three-month-old babies smile longer at faces that adults find attractive.

Teacher: So who judges what's beautiful and what isn't?

Maggie: We didn't really go into that, but it seems that perceptions of beauty are connected to health and fertility. In some places people go for shiny hair, in other cultures women use mascara to make their eyes look bigger and to give themselves a younger look, but a universal indicator of being young and healthy is to have clear skin.

Mike: And that's why so much money is made from skin cleansers, moisturisers, facial creams and so on.

Teacher: Well, there are certainly plenty of tricks to this trade.

Maggie: Yeah, and most of them aren't new tricks at all. I think I could make a link at this part of the presentation to what Mike was saying about the early 20th century, because there's a trend now in the beauty industry to go back to the approach they had a century ago, when they stressed a connection between beauty and health. They got women to have facials and do exercise classes. Now they aim at beauty, but also like people to be fit, not just thin.

Mike: Oh, come on! The industry just scares people into going on diets that can actually harm them. And most of those thin models aren't in good physical condition, they're just hungry.

Maggie: You can't tell just by looking. Anyway, I'm not denying that image is important. In fact, beauty firms spend up to 25% of their turnover on advertising.

Teacher: That's incredible!

Maggie: Isn't it! And they put just 2 or 3% into research and development. By comparison, in the pharmaceutical industry, 15% of sales goes into research and development.

Teacher: Well, it sounds like you have got the topic well covered. I'm sure the class will really enjoy your presentation.

That is the end of Section 3. You now have half a minute to check your answers.

Now turn to Section 4.

Section 4

You will hear a talk by an archaeological scientist on her latest research. First, you have some time to look at questions 31 to 40.

Now listen and answer questions 31 to 40.

Good morning, ladies and gentlemen. Many of you may remember that in 1991 a couple who were hiking high in the mountains on the border between Italy and Austria found the body of a man who had died 5,300 years ago.

This corpse was later given the nickname 'the Iceman'. Fortunately, a complete set of clothes and a variety of gear were found on or near the corpse, and these give us further clues as to his identity. Today I'd like to speak to you about some of the latest findings on the Iceman.

Scientists have learned from the Iceman's corpse in the same way as detectives investigating a murder gather clues from the victim's body. The study of the Iceman's bones shows that he was 46 years old at the time of death, which is relatively old for people at that time. It appears that he belonged to a group from central northern Europe rather than to the group of people who lived not far to the south of the spot where his body was found. Yet it seems he may have moved around somewhat during his life. Although exactly where he spent his life is unknown, investigation of his tooth enamel suggests that he grew up in one place and then spent several decades in another area.

Samples taken from his stomach and intestines give us an indication of what he'd eaten shortly before his death, including grains, though this does not allow conclusions to be drawn as to what he usually ate. However, samples of his hair show that his usual diet consisted of plants and the meat of several animals. Living in a time long before the development of modern medicine, the tattoos on his back may indicate acupuncture points, yet on the other hand they could simply be a form of body decoration. It seems that he was not in a good state of health in the last six months of his life. There are three lines known as Beau's lines on the single fingernail that was found. These lines occur if the nail stops growing due to illness and then starts growing again.

It was initially assumed that he had died of the cold in autumn because of the presence of a piece of fruit that ripens in late summer. Yet there is now strong botanical evidence that he died in spring. This is because pollen of the hop hornbeam tree was found in his intestines, and that small tree blooms only in late spring. So he may have breathed some in or drunk some water containing the pollen shortly before his death.

So, what else do we know about the Iceman? He ate a primitive form of wheat, which was baked into bread on an open fire. Although leaves of moss were found in his intestines, it appears that moss was not part of his diet but had probably entered his mouth by accident. In those days the local people had no paper bags or plastic wrapping, and so used moss to pack food in. Moss was a very versatile plant, with different varieties that grew far to the north being used by the Vikings as toilet paper.

The equipment found around the body gives us many clues as to his way of life. He was well prepared for climbing through the mountains: he had a jacket made from deer hide and goat hide, and a pair of shoes made from the skin of both goat and bear and then insulated with plant material. Over the top of it all he was wearing a cape made from grass and bast, which is made from bark. This could give us a clue as to his occupation. In fact, this cape resembles capes still worn by shepherds in the Balkans, and the site where he was found is near an area where shepherds traditionally take their flocks in summer. Yet the theory that he was a shepherd has little else to support it. It's been proposed that he was a hunter due to the fact that he was carrying a bow and some arrows. Some earlier ideas that he was a warrior or a trader of flint have been abandoned for lack of any supporting material.

The Iceman was found lying on a large rock, and so it was believed initially that he had fallen asleep on the rock and then died. However, the consensus now is that he died nearby and then floated into that position during periods when the ice thawed. There are several indicators for this: first, the awkward position of his left arm; second, the position of his right hand, which was stuck under another rock; third, the missing outer layer of skin; and the fact that some of his belongings were a few metres from the body.

Despite these interesting findings, there are still many things that we don't know about the Iceman. What was he doing up there high in the mountains, apparently by himself? Did he die from exhaustion and cold while running away from danger? We may never know exactly what the cause of death was, because this would require an autopsy, which has not been allowed as it would cause too much damage to the corpse. When the body was first removed, it was thought to be that of a missing mountain climber, and a number of people disturbed the site, wrecking a good part of the evidence in the process. But, hopefully, with further research we will be able to solve some of the mysteries that still surround the Iceman, who has already taught us so much about the way of life at that time.

That is the end of Section 4. You now have half a minute to check your answers.

That is the end of the Listening Test. You now have ten minutes to transfer your answers to the answer sheet.

Listening Test 4

You will hear four different recordings and you will have to answer questions on what you hear.

There will be time for you to read the instructions and questions before the recording is played.

You will also have the opportunity to check your answers.

The recordings will be played ONCE only.

The test is in four sections. Write your answers on the question sheet as you listen. At the end of Section 4, you have ten minutes to transfer your answers onto the answer sheet, which is on page 31. When you finish, check the answers at the back of the book.

Now turn to Section 1.

Section 1

A woman has just arrived at a shopping mall with her children. You will hear her talking to a man at the information desk. First, you have some time to look at questions 1 to 6 and the floor plan of the shopping mall.

Now listen and answer questions 1 to 6.

Man: Good morning, can I help you?

Woman: Yes. I've never been here before and I've just got a few questions about where a few places are here.

Man: Fine. Here's a floor plan of the mall, you can take that with you, but if you have any questions, I'd be very happy to help.

Woman: Well, I'm afraid I always find these floor plans a bit confusing, so could you just show me exactly where we are on this?

Man: No problem. Here we are at the information desk, right in the middle, next to the escalators.

The man says they are at the information desk and that it is in the middle, next to the escalator. Therefore, 'C' has been written next to the example on the question paper. Now continue with questions 1 to 6.

Woman: Right. Now, I heard there's a children's play centre where you can leave your children while you do the shopping.

Man: That's right. You can see it on the floor plan; it's in the corner, to the left of the supermarket. There are plenty of toys for them to play with there – also, there's fresh fruit to eat and they can have fun with the other children.

Woman: Sounds good, doesn't it, kids? I was thinking I might take them to have their hair cut first. Is that the <u>hairdresser between the furniture shop and the children's clothes shop</u>?

Man: Yes, it is. They do children's haircuts as well.

Woman: Oh, lovely. Now, my little boy's going to a friend's birthday party next week, and we wanted to buy a present. Do you know if there are any stores that might have things a seven-year-old boy would like?

Man: Oh yes, <u>there's a toy store right next to the shoe shop</u>. They've got a good range of toys. I'm sure you'll find something for a child of that age. I often buy things there myself. The prices are quite reasonable.

Woman: Oh, that's good to hear. Oh, and also, are there any toilets on this floor?

Man: Yes, they're in a bit of a hidden corner. You just go <u>past the bookstore</u> – you can see they sell newspapers there too – <u>and down the corridor</u>.

Woman: Ah, yes, I see. I'd better take them there before we go to the hairdresser. What else do I need to do? Oh yeah, I've got to buy some credit for my mobile phone. Can I do that at the <u>phone kiosk over there near those benches</u>?

Man: Yes, you can. You can also do it at the supermarket if you want.

Woman: Right. Now, we've just come up from the car park, but we took the escalator. I might have a lot of things to carry later on, so I was wondering if there's an elevator.

Man: Yes, it's <u>next to the computer store, near the top of the stairs</u>.

Woman: Oh yes, I can see it now.

Before you hear the rest of the conversation, you have some time to look at questions 7 to 10.

Now listen and answer questions 7 to 10.

Woman: Oh, when I parked the car I couldn't see how much you have to pay for parking.

Man: It's free for the first two hours, but after that it's $3 an hour.

Woman: Hmm. I think with all the things we have to do, we might be here for more than two hours. So if you park there for three hours altogether, you have to pay $3, and <u>if it's four hours, you pay $6</u> and so on.

Man: Yes, that's right.

Woman: Uh-huh. How about the children's play centre. Is there any charge for leaving your children there?

Man: Oh no, that's a free service of the shopping mall. However, there's a policy that the children have to be <u>at least 18 months old</u>.

Woman: My youngest is just 10 months old, but I'd rather keep her with me anyway. Also, we might need to get something to eat later. Is there any place to buy lunch?

Man: Oh yes, you can get all kinds of things at the food court, from snacks to fast food to healthy meals. There's a really good range. <u>It's two floors up on level five</u>. It's best to take the elevator.

Woman: Do you know if they have pizza? Both my kids really love pizza.

Man: Yes, they do. Oh, did you know you can watch a movie here, too?

Woman: Yes, I've heard <u>there's a cinema on the top floor</u>. There might be something on that my kids'd be interested in.

Man: Yeah, there are a couple of children's films on at the moment.

Woman: Well, thank you very much; you've been a great help.

Man: My pleasure.

That is the end of Section 1. You now have half a minute to check your answers.

Now turn to Section 2.

Section 2

You will hear a talk by a representative of an agency that finds people to look after homes when their owners are away. He is talking to a group of homeowners. First, you have some time to look at questions 11 to 20.

Now listen and answer questions 11 to 20.

Good evening, ladies and gentlemen, I'm glad you've been able to make it to this introductory talk about our agency, which is called Contented Homes. My name's Gary and I'm going to explain what our business involves, but first I'd like to tell you something about the background of our agency.

We commenced operations <u>back in 1989</u>, and essentially our job is to find suitable people to live in and look after other people's homes while they're away. The homeowners – people like yourselves – might be away on holidays or temporarily working in another city or country, and they want to be sure that while they're away, their home will be secure, and that when they come back, everything will be in good condition. When we first started out, we conducted most of our business over the phone, but now the bulk of it is done <u>over the Internet</u>.

Basically, this is how it works: homeowners come to us when they need to find reliable, trustworthy people to take good care of their home for a limited period of time. The people who stay in your home and take care of it are called 'housesitters'. The housesitters live at your place for periods of anything between <u>one month</u> and two years.

There are all kinds of reasons why people housesit. Some are couples, others are single. Often they're saving up to buy their own home, or they may be renovating their own home and just need somewhere to stay temporarily, or they might have just moved to your city. Although <u>housesitters don't pay you any rent</u> when they're living in your home, they are required to pay any bills for the telephone, gas, electricity and so on. So, for the homeowner, this is not a way to make money.

When someone registers with us to become a housesitter, they provide us with some of their personal details such as their age and occupation. I need to stress here that our agency *does not* carry out a security check on the people who have registered with us to be housesitters. Many housesitters have references from people whose houses or apartments they've looked after in the past. <u>It's up to you to check those references</u>. Allowing someone to live in your home is not a decision to be taken lightly, so we also recommend that you meet with any prospective housesitters and interview them before deciding which person or people would be most suitable to look after your home in your absence.

There are similarities between housesitters and tenants, but there are differences as well. <u>Housesitters don't have as many rights</u> as people who have a lease on a property. As the homeowner, you can give a spare set of keys to your home to a neighbour, friend or relative. That person's allowed to drop in on the housesitters without prior notice at any time – within reason – to check that the house is in order, and the housesitters aren't allowed to stop them from entering.

There are many good reasons to use the services of a housesitter. Burglars soon notice when people are away, so theft is much less likely if someone is living in your home. But it's not simply a matter of security. Housesitters keep your home clean and tidy. Some of them are even more houseproud than the actual owners. In addition, many people need a housesitter to look after pets and keep the garden in order.

Now I'd like tell you about the fees we charge. First, *you* the homeowners don't have to pay us anything. When people who want to be housesitters come to us, they have to pay $375 to go into our directory. That's where we get the money to run our service. As I said, we don't check to see that the information supplied by them is correct; it would simply cost us far too much time and money to do that.

When you've decided that you want to go ahead and have a housesitter look after your home, we definitely think it's a good idea for you to take out insurance for your home. You'll find that many insurance companies prefer the higher degree of security if someone's living in your home than if it's left empty. Anyway, I hope I've given you a clear idea of our service, and now I'd be happy to take any questions.

That is the end of Section 2. You now have half a minute to check your answers.

Now turn to Section 3.

Section 3

You will hear two students talking to their teacher about a seminar paper they are preparing for their Population Studies class.

First, you have some time to look at questions 21 to 25.

Now listen and answer questions 21 to 25.

Teacher: So, how's your seminar paper going?

Woman: Oh, it's almost ready. My head's just full of statistics at the moment.

Teacher: Is there anything you found particularly interesting?

Man: Yeah, for instance, about where people choose to live when they migrate to Australia. The focus of our talk is on migration to Sydney, but we found we needed to look briefly at migration to other parts of Australia as well.

Woman: Hmm. Most migrants go to the big cities, but it isn't the same for all nationalities. For instance, over the last five years, with the British, only about one third of them altogether went to Sydney and Melbourne.

Teacher: So, where did most of them go?

Man: Oh, all over the place, but for some reason quite a few ended up over in Perth.

Teacher: That's not a bad place to live.

Man: No. But with the Chinese, 26% of them choose to live in Melbourne and 58% in Sydney.

Teacher: Really? Do you have any idea why the Chinese and British have such different settlement patterns?

Man: Well, not really. Sometimes it's hard to find out exactly why people choose to live where they do. There's a thriving Lebanese community in Melbourne, but more than seven out of ten people from Lebanon were drawn to Sydney.

Teacher: I see. So you've covered groups from Europe, East Asia and the Middle East. Do you have anything on people from other regions?

Woman: Yes. When we went through data from the Department of Immigration and the Bureau of Statistics, we found that in the case of the <u>Malaysians</u>, for some reason only <u>a minority chose Sydney and Melbourne</u>, but I don't know exactly where most of them ended up. I think quite a few of them were attracted to Queensland because of the climate.

Teacher: Yeah, it must be hard for people coming from a tropical region to get used to colder winters. What about the New Zealanders?

Man: Well, they don't need a visa for Australia, so they're counted separately from all other nationalities, but <u>the vast bulk of them have ended up in Sydney</u>. You'd think that Melbourne'd be more to their liking because its climate's more like what they're used to and the distance from New Zealand to Melbourne is about the same.

Before you hear the rest of the conversation, you have some time to look at questions 26 to 30.

Now listen and answer questions 26 to 30.

Teacher: You also looked into *why* people choose the places they do, didn't you?

Woman: Yes. Well, people often go where the work is. I mean, it's no use finding a nice place to live if you're going to be unemployed. But there's a more decisive factor, and that is that <u>people generally like to live near their friends and relatives, and with people from their own country, so they won't be so isolated</u>. And they do that despite the higher housing prices in the larger cities.

Teacher: Yeah, rents are getting ridiculous. But hasn't Sydney always attracted people – I mean, even people born elsewhere in Australia?

Woman: Well, historically that was the case, but even though Sydney's grown a lot recently, there's been hardly any increase in the number of Australian-born people living in Sydney.

Teacher: Why is that? I mean, I can understand why people would be leaving; a lot of people feel Sydney's getting too crowded and hectic.

Woman: But that can't be the reason because they often end up in places such as south-east Queensland, where the infrastructure simply isn't coping with the rapid population growth and faster pace of life.

Man: The research shows that the ones leaving Sydney are particularly middle-aged and elderly people who own the place they live in. By selling their Sydney home when they retire and buying and living in a cheaper one elsewhere, <u>they then have more funds left over</u>.

Teacher: It must be difficult making that shift at their age.

Woman: I think moving or migrating's hard for *anyone*.

Teacher: Quite right. But what effect is migration having?

Woman: Well, there are all kinds of effects, but sociologists talk about a growing gap between Sydney and Melbourne on the one hand, and the rest of the country on the other. You see, the most recent data shows that <u>60% of the overseas arrivals went to those two cities</u>, even though Sydney and Melbourne combined have got just 40% of the country's population.

Teacher: But you've got to remember that Australia is one of the most urbanised countries in the world. A good 50% of the population live in the state capitals, not including the urban fringes. Is anything being done to promote growth in other regions?

Man: Well, the government's got several proposals. We need more people in rural areas, but no one's suggesting that we encourage farmers to migrate to Australia because agriculture's very capital-intensive in this country. But the government's <u>thinking about having lower tax rates on private firms that employ newly arrived migrants in towns outside Sydney and Melbourne.</u> Of course, these days the government doesn't want to actually provide jobs for them but they are willing to favour employers who employ them.

Teacher: Do you think that'd work?

Woman: I don't know. There's nothing to stop them moving to one of the two big cities if they feel like it.

Teacher: Exactly.

Woman: In fact, the statistics don't give the full picture. When they migrate, people very often initially live outside of Sydney, so in the statistics they're recorded as having settled outside Sydney. <u>But then after a while many make the move to Sydney. So the real picture's even more out of balance than what the statistics say.</u>

Teacher: Statistics really can be a slippery thing sometimes, can't they?

Woman: That's for sure.

That is the end of Section 3. You now have half a minute to check your answers.

Now turn to Section 4.

Section 4

Emma Bell is an agricultural scientist. In the following lecture she describes some of the advantages of the hemp plant. First, you have some time to look at questions 31 to 40.

Now listen and answer questions 31 to 40.

When we think of progress, we tend to look to the future. However, the past can also provide inspiration. Today I'd like to outline some of the many ways in which the hemp plant – a plant that was used very widely until the early 20th century – can benefit both humans and the environment.

You may remember that when the use of computers became more widespread, there was much talk of the 'paperless office', yet now far more paper is being used than ever before. Most of that paper is made from wood, but it can also be made from hemp. Hemp is a fast-growing annual plant that can be <u>harvested within four months</u> of germination, whereas a tree takes 20 years. This means that a hectare of hemp can produce 80 times as much paper as a hectare of trees. In fact, hemp was the main source for paper production until the 20th century and the paper it makes is of superior quality to that made from wood. Many of the rivers in the vicinity of today's paper mills suffer the effects of pollution from bleach and other chemicals used in the manufacture of paper from wood. In contrast, <u>paper made from hemp does not require bleach.</u>

So much clothing these days is made from cotton. Yet fabric has been made from hemp for over 7,000 years. The trouble with cotton crops is that they take a heavy toll on the environment and are often dependent on irrigation. Hemp can grow <u>using far less water</u> and does not need as much fertiliser or pesticides. In fact, hemp crops even have a natural resistance to pests. Clothes made from the tough fibre of hemp also last longer than those made from cotton, which is not something that'll make clothing manufacturers very happy. But another way in which hemp is the superior material is that it's more effective in <u>blocking out UV rays</u> from the sun, which can cause <u>skin cancer</u>. To top it off, clothing made from hemp is very comfortable to wear.

In parts of the world that still don't have electricity, this versatile plant can also be used to light lamps. Back in the days of sailing ships, when hemp was used to make ropes and sails, lamps were often fuelled by <u>whale oil</u>, which gave off a much stronger-smelling black smoke. The pursuit of that oil was one of the reasons for the existence of the whaling industry, which hunted many species of whale almost to extinction.

Closer to our own time, Henry Ford used hemp in the production of his first cars. These days, with panels being made of metal, even a minor accident can lead to costly repairs. Being derived from a plant, <u>hemp panels would be less expensive</u>. Yet perhaps an even more significant consequence would be that, instead of old cars being left to rust by the roadside, an abandoned car made from hemp would rot faster. A further advantage in the case of automobiles is the fuel. One of the major causes of global warming is the use of fossil fuels in cars and trucks. Methanol is an alternative to petrol, and it can be extracted from hemp. This fuel is already used by racing cars, and it <u>doesn't produce as much air pollution</u>, thus placing a smaller burden on the air we breathe.

Hemp is also a source for a variety of foods. The oil that is obtained from the plant can be used to make cooking oil, butter, cheese and even ice-cream. <u>Flour</u> derived from hemp has a greater protein content than normal wheat flour, and its seeds contain all the amino acids, providing a form of protein that's more easily digested than that in soybeans.

Carpets made from hemp are more durable than other carpets and are resistant to mildew, which grows in humid or damp conditions. It can also be used in the home to produce furnishings such as fibreboard, furniture and even plastics. Paints and varnish made from petrochemicals <u>contain poisons, whereas this is not the case with those produced from hemp</u>.

Hemp plants are best grown close together, and because they produce an abundance of leaves, the ground underneath the plants is shaded, which hinders the growth of weeds, so farmers don't have to spend money on potentially dangerous herbicides. It thrives in areas with <u>low rainfall</u> and may be useful in combating salinity because it doesn't need irrigation and its long taproot can reach underground nutrients and water.

As a fast-growing plant, it's an easily renewable, biodegradable and ecologically sustainable source of a vast range of products that are currently made from polluting resources such as coal, metals, gas and oil. This is quite plainly a case where we can make progress by learning from the past.

That is the end of Section 4. You now have half a minute to check your answers.

That is the end of the Listening Test. You now have ten minutes to transfer your answers to the answer sheet.

Answer key

LISTENING

Symbols used in the Listening answer key

/ If there is more than one possible word or phrase within an answer, this is shown by the symbol /. For instance, 'less pollution/polluting' means that the answer can be 'less pollution' or 'less polluting'.

// In some cases there is more than one correct answer. This is indicated by the symbol //. For instance, 'all universities // every university' means that the answer can be 'all universities' or 'every university'.

( ) If part of the answer is given in brackets, this means that the word or words in brackets are optional. For instance, 'half (an) hour' means that the answer can be 'half hour' or 'half an hour'.

Listening Test 1

SECTION 1

1 Penny Ryan
2 24 March 1982 // March 24(,) 1982 // 24.(0)3.(19)82 // (0)3.24.(19)82
3 Blacktown // Black Town
4 7690 3275
5 monthly // every month // once a month
6 A   7 C   8 B
9 B   10 A

SECTION 2

11 shoes
12 beach cafe
13 7 (am/a.m.) to/till/until/– 6 (pm/p.m.) // 7 to 6 // 7–6
14 twice a/per week // Tuesday(s) and Friday(s)
15 on (the/your) balcony/balconies
16 birds, fish
17 11 (pm/p.m.) // 11 at night
18 A, E   19 B, D   20 D, E

SECTION 3

21 B   22 A   23 D   24 E
25 F   26 C   27 C   28 B
29 A   30 B

SECTION 4

31 (nomadic) lifestyle // nomadism
32 clothes/clothing
33 milk, meat   34 gardening
35 feed // eat   36 salt
37 C   38 C   39 A   40 B

Listening Test 2

SECTION 1

1 (Class) C/c // C/c license
2 28 River   3 3701 8699
4 student card   5 (by) cash
6 C   7 B   8 B
9 C   10 A

SECTION 2

11 B   12 F   13 C   14 G
15 D   16 D   17 E   18 G
19 A   20 F

SECTION 3

21 B   22 B   23 A   24 B
25 B   26 C   27 D   28 C
29 B   30 H

SECTION 4

31 reason(s) // motivation(s)
32 funding limitations // funds limited// limited funds/funding
33 85%
34 exercise, therapy
35 computer games
36 reduce stress
37 personal development
38 B   39 B   40 A

Listening Test 3

SECTION 1

1 room service
2 waiter
3 Tourism Management
4 French, Korean
5, 6, 7 *In any order:* B, F, G (clear away plates, take luggage to rooms, work in hotel bar)
8, 9, 10 *In any order:* C, D, G (medical insurance, parking, uniforms)

SECTION 2

11 A, E
12 B, D
13 four/4 months/mths
14 75%
15 (on/via/through) the Internet // online
16 $6,000
17 passport photos
18 $435
19 working days
20 interview

SECTION 3

21 C   22 A   23 B   24 C
25 B   26 A   27 C   28 A
29 C   30 A

SECTION 4

31 B   32 H   33 D   34 C
35 E   36 A   37 C   38 B
39 A   40 B

Listening Test 4

SECTION 1

1 A   2 H   3 I   4 G
5 D   6 F
7 $6 // $6.00 // six dollars
8 eighteen/18 months // 1½ years
9 (on) (level/floor) five/5 // (the) fifth/5th (level/floor)
10 (a) cinema/theatre

SECTION 2

11 1989
12 Internet
13 one/1 month
14 rent
15 reference(s)
16 rights
17 theft/thieves // burglary/burglar(s)
18 pet(s), garden(s)
19 $375
20 (home) insurance

SECTION 3

21 C   22 B   23 B   24 C
25 B   26 B   27 C   28 C
29 A   30 A

SECTION 4

31 4/four months
32 bleach
33 water/irrigation
34 skin cancer // UV/ultraviolet rays
35 whale oil // oil from/of whales
36 less expensive // cheaper
37 (air) pollution
38 C   39 E   40 A

READING

Note: Italicised text in parentheses presents clues from the texts.

Reading Test 1

SECTION 1

1 E; (*City of Windyhill presents Free Organic Lunch*)

2 H; (*Step out with your partner at the Happy Valley Ballroom and show off your moves, from the Jitterbug to the Jive.*)

3 B; (*All aspects of practical film-making taught*)

4 F; (*Modern Theatre Company*)

5 3, 3; (*change your PIN*)

6 1, 1; (*account balances*)

7 2, 1; (*make a payment*)

8 2, 3; (*delete from billing list*)

9 3, 1; (*order a statement*)

10 3, 5; (*speak to a customer service officer*)

11 summer (*need to take special care during the bushfire season, which is summer*)

12 campfires (*Apart from obvious precautions such as not lighting campfires, not smoking outside ...*)

13 overalls (*long-sleeved overalls or a long-sleeved wool or cotton shirt and long pants*)

14 leather (*sturdy shoes or boots with enclosed toes, preferably leather*)

SECTION 2

15 FALSE; (*possibility of extension*)

16 TRUE; (*help our elderly and disabled clients integrate into society*)

17 TRUE; (*the successful applicant will be required to assist with reviewing and developing further initiatives as part of WellFare's strategic plan*)

18 NOT GIVEN; the job involves helping disabled people but vision-impaired people are not specifically mentioned.

19 FALSE; (*To be considered ... you will need to have a degree in a relevant discipline*)

20 NOT GIVEN; sick leave is not mentioned in the text.

21 TRUE; (*A requirement of this position is a satisfactory police records check.*)

22 F; (*Failure to comply with any aspect of this policy may result in dismissal from the Company.*)

23 C; (*Office workers who smoke are provided with a balcony ... employees may smoke on Company premises outdoors*)

24 B; (*from 1 January next year ... all employees are required to respect the Company's policy*)

25 E; (*Smoking in offices is forbidden at all times.*)

26 A; (*the Company is increasingly aware of the need for a new policy on smoking in the workplace, for the health of both smokers and non-smokers among employees.*)

27 F; (*If you have any queries about this policy, please address them to Julio Santos, HR or your team leader.*)

28 D; (*Extra bins have been provided especially for this purpose and using them will make the working environment more pleasant for everyone.*)

SECTION 3

29 vi; (*the country has been faced with the threat of major floods for most of its existence.*)

30 viii; (*Over the centuries they have planned to augment the available land, protecting the low-lying areas by building bigger and better dykes*)

31 v; (*the Dutch have not waited*)

32 ix; (*The Dutch see that such a plan is vital for their own protection*)

33 iii; (*Sand dug out from the North Sea will be added in vast quantities to many coastal areas*)

34 i; (*There appear to be at least three main commercial spin-offs to the project*)
Note: Items ii, iv and vii are distractors.

35 C; (*With something like one-third of its land surface below sea level*)

36 B; (*they still attract tourists*)

37 D; (*the rest of the world cannot be relied upon to agree on a policy in time to give seriously threatened nations such as themselves a chance to take effective countermeasures*)

38 A; (*There are no plans to build all dykes higher and stronger, as might be expected; indeed, many of the dykes will be taken down*)

39 B; (*Along the North Sea coast, beach expansion will extend the land seawards by up to a kilometre*)

40 B; (*... as will part of the Netherlands' very generous civil service pension fund*)

Reading Test 2

SECTION 1

1 F; (*This course is designed for younger students ... whose native language is not English.*)

2 E; (*for those students in Years 8–10 who have had difficulties in understanding mathematical concepts*)

3 A; (*This course is for those who expect to start a French course*)

4 B; (*The Senior Physics course will suit those students who ... wish to study Physics at senior level*)

5 F; (*Days: Mon/Wed/Fri*)

6 10; (*The walk is 10 km in total.*)

7 8; (*Cost is $8.00*)

8 9; (*Please meet ... from 9 am.*)

9 FALSE; (*Anyone can join the library – it's free.*)

10 NOT GIVEN; there is no mention of passwords.

11 TRUE; (*If you're under 18 you will need to have the application form signed by a parent or guardian.*)

12 FALSE; (*You can borrow up to 25 items at a time.*)

13 TRUE; (*Items reserved by another member cannot be renewed.*)

14 NOT GIVEN; no reference is made to waiting/ordering in advance.

SECTION 2

15 iv; (*Frankstown Books ... is seeking to appoint an auditor*)

16 ii; (*must have been with Frankstown Books for at least two years and will have a tertiary accounting or business degree*)

17 vii; (*and supply a letter of referral from this manager as well as written recommendations from staff in two other departments.*)

18 ix; (*Applicants must be prepared to be called for an interview between 23 and 26 February*)

19 vi; (*It is expected that the position will be upgraded to a senior position*)

20 i; (*The position carries an allowance of $17,120 in addition to the salary already paid*)

21 iii; (*contact Sally Jones on Extension 78 in the Human Relations Office*)
    Note: Items v, viii and x are distractors.

22 viruses; (*There have been difficulties reported to management over the last two weeks regarding viruses*)

23 staff; (*Management is reluctant to do this as it would reduce the number of staff that can be employed.*)

24 (formal) (work) breaks; (*staff are required to limit their private use of emails and Net surfing to formal work breaks*)

25 breach of contract; (*Conducting private business during working hours constitutes a breach of contract*)

26 business; (*An employee of another local business has recently been dismissed for downloading illegal material*)

27 illegal material; (*illegal material on a staff member's computer*)

28 criminal charges; (*will be reported to the police for possible criminal charges*)

SECTION 3

29 minerals and algae; (*many tiny gem-coloured lakes – some purple, some orange from minerals and algae.*)

30 mineral residues; (*scientists have been able to map the location of mineral residues from ancient lakes and springs*)

31 (the) Saharan pump; (*This back-and-forth migration is called the Saharan pump*)

32 rock art; (*Rock art suggests they had already made the transition from hunting to raising livestock.*)

33 (Underground) canals; (*Underground canals tapped into groundwater and directed it to fields without loss to evaporation*)

34 A; (*almost all of its six million people live huddled on the Mediterranean coast*)

35 C; (*Lake Megafezzan, gleamed here about 200,000 years ago, when rainfall was abundant*)

36 A; (*Human communities have pulsed here ... When moist eras visited, they thrived. When the dry times returned they shrank or collapsed.*)

37 D; (*About 5,000 years ago the rains stopped once more, the lakes disappeared, and the deserts took hold. Yet this time the people stayed.*)

38 C; (*they were a sedentary people living off savana agriculture.*)

39 C; (*And then the 'fossil' water, stored up in wet times, started to give out and the civilization collapsed.*)

40 B; (*for the humans who have lived in Libya for thousands of years, it has been a corridor.*)

Reading Test 3

SECTION 1

1 (by) bus; (*passengers will be taken by bus on to Launceford*)

2 (at) 11.42 am; (*will travel via Harringby, arriving at Launceford at 11.42 am*)

3 (at) Bickley; (*The 1.40 express ... will pause at Bickley to allow passengers to get off and travel on by bus to Launceford.*)

4 (at) 5 pm; (*The 3.55 and 5.25 to Launceford ... arriving at 5 pm and 6.30 pm respectively.*)

5 D; (*hand-sewing ... dressmaking*)

6 E; (*$110 plus materials*)

7 C; (*A revision class to brush up those steps will be held at 7 pm. When: every Wednesday 8 pm – 10.30 pm*)

8 A; (*The exercises are especially useful for adults whose occupation requires long periods of sitting at a desk.*)

9 C; (*Dance New Vogue, Latin and Modern to delightful music*)

10 B; (*earn a little extra pocket money*)

11 (a) security scare; (*A recent attempt by a staff member to enter company premises last weekend caused a security scare.*)

12 completing unfinished business; (*Any staff member ... may stay for the purpose of completing unfinished business*)

13 (at) hourly (intervals); (*buildings and car park are patrolled at hourly intervals*)

14 any suspicious activity; (*immediately report any suspicious activity to the security office at any time*)

SECTION 2

15 iii; (*experience in footwear studies ... report on developments in the trade.*)

16 vii; (*No experience is necessary, as on-the-job training will be given in the use of hand and machine tools, stitching and soling.*)

17 viii; (*in charge of staffing*)

18 iv; (*basic typing and shorthand skills as well as knowledge of common clerical practices.*)

19 v; (*to maintain the cleanliness of the building.*)

20 x; (*position of responsibility ... supervise the leatherworkers*)

21 i; (*experience in assessing the soundness of products*)

22 G; (*Upgraded qualifications ... will be taken into consideration with regard to salaries.*)

23 D; (*for a qualification that benefits the employee and is in the Company's interest.*)

24 B; (*Leave from company duties may be granted in the case of successful applicants for external training for a maximum of two days per week*)

25 C; (*A staff member who leaves within this time frame will forfeit any holiday pay.*)

26 FALSE; (*the board's decision will be final and not open to further negotiation.*)

27 TRUE; (*a recommendation must be ... signed by the Head of Department*)

28 FALSE; (*The company will contribute 50% of the cost for external training*)

29 NOT GIVEN; there is no mention of a preference for university degrees.

SECTION 3

30 C; (*They are, like ants, social insects and live in colonies comprising various castes in nests.*)

31 H; (*Some termite mounds can reach an impressive 6 metres tall and several metres across*)

32 D; (*workers that cannot reproduce, fly or see*)

33 F; (*She grows into an large, egg-laying machine about 30 millimetres in diameter*)

34 B; (*They are also a useful source of food for birds, lizards, many other small mammals*)

35 C; (*Termites are the same size as ants and are often referred to as 'white ants', but they are not actually ants: the ant has a very thin waist whereas a termite does not.*)

36 A; (*A termite colony normally consists of a queen and king who together are the primary reproductive insects / A small number of young will develop to become queens or kings ... these are called alates*)

37 C; (*The new king and queen ... seal themselves into a small chamber, and then after a few days the queen will begin to lay her eggs.*)

38 D; (*Worker termites ... gather food, ... feed the rest of the colony, themselves and the soldiers. They also repair any damage done to the nest*)

39 C; (*keeping stacks of timber and firewood dry and away from the house*)

40 D; D summarises the whole topic.

Reading Test 4

SECTION 1

1 Channel 2 (7.30 *German cooking series / 9.00 French with subtitles*)

2 Channel 1 (10.30 *Horror film, MA – Mature audience, not suited for children under 15*)

3 *Get Rich Quick.* (Channel 3, 7.00, *General knowledge quiz with money prizes*)

4 *Simon Says* (Channel 2, 7.15, *Humorous comment on the news*)

5 *You Look Good!* (Channel 3, 8.00, *Series on beauty tips*)

6 *Pet Care* (Channel 1, 10.10, *Looking after pets*)

7 G/General; (Channel 2, 7.30, *Was Koche Ich?*; 8.30, *Cities of the World*)

8 growers/farmers; (*all sold directly by the growers*)

9 across the state; (*Farmers show up from across the state.*)

10 quality of produce; (*the quality of produce is their main priority*)

11 plastic bag; (*The market is plastic bag free, so bring your own baskets, bags and trolleys.*)

12 Auckland Primary School; (*St Bernadette's Reserve (right behind Auckland Primary School)*)

13 (market) manager; (*For more information on market operations and stalls, email the manager*)

14 mailing list; (*To be added to the St Bernadette Farmers' Market mailing list and receive a reminder email*)

SECTION 2

15 G; (*The Mossville hospital ... is located in the centre of the city of Mossville.*)
Note: C is wrong because there is no mention of a research facility.

16 F; (*St Aldan's Hospital is ... associated with the University of Victoria and with Mossville University.*)

17 D; (*Workers in the field of aged care will appreciate the Davidson Centre*)

18 B; (*It offers maternity services, and has a children's department*)

19 E; (*Extensive staff education and development programs are provided*)

20 43; (*Belford Health has over 43 sites*)

21 1887; (*the history of the Mossville hospital dates back to 1887*)

22 1,025; (*Belford Health provides 1,025 beds throughout its numerous sites*)

23 TRUE; (*accepted provided that they include a minimum of 12 weeks supervised teaching practice / a Master's or PhD degree in Education that does not include teaching practice is not acceptable*)

24 NOT GIVEN; there is no reference in the text to teachers' choice of sports training.

25 FALSE; (*wearing jeans and a T-shirt is unacceptable on school premises, although at school camps such informal clothing is acceptable.*)

26 TRUE; (*extra allowances paid ... for years of teaching experience.*)

27 FALSE; (*All teachers in Years 11 and 12 will be required to make themselves available to teach at least one other subject aside from their major subject area.*)

28 NOT GIVEN; the relative contributions of government and private donations are not compared.

SECTION 3

29 power; (*From its first discovery, it has symbolized wealth and power.*)

30 obsession; (*Gold has caused obsession in men and nations*)

31 the Middle East; (*Archaeological digs suggest the use of gold began in the Middle East*)

32 coffin; (*They uncovered a gold coffin whose quality showed the advanced state of Egyptian craftsmanship and goldworking.*)

33 Animal art; (*Persian gold work is most famous for its animal art*)

34 emperor; (*the citizens of Rome wore necklaces that contained coins with the image of the emperor.*)

35 D; (*the skill of pre-Columbian cultures in the use of gold was highly advanced long before the arrival of the Spanish. Native goldsmiths had mastered most of the techniques known by their European*)

contemporaries when the Spanish arrived in 1492.)

36 B; (*Gold also has extraordinarily high reflective powers that are relied upon in the shielding that protects spaceships and satellites from solar radiation, and in industrial and medical lasers that use gold-coated reflectors*)

37 A; (*Because gold is biologically inactive, it has become a vital tool for medical research*)

38 A; (*Demand ... increases during periods of world crisis or instability*)

39 B; (*Investment gold is therefore an excellent hedge against inflation, and protects earnings for the future.*)

40 D; the first five paragraphs outline the history of gold and the remaining three explain some of its uses.

WRITING

Writing Test 1

Sample responses

Task 1

Dear Sir/Madam,

The recent changes in the train timetable have caused me some problems. For the past four years I have been taking the 7.43, but it no longer stops at Bexland, and I must now either wait for the 7.57 or catch the earlier 7.15 to my work.

With the new timetable, if I wait for the 7.57, I arrive late for work, but if I catch the earlier 7.15, I must walk around the city for half an hour or go for a coffee before I can get into my office. This also makes me rather tired in the morning and I am less effective at work. I have spoken to other passengers at Bexland who agree with me that the new timetable is unsatisfactory.

I would therefore ask for an adjustment of the new timetable so that the 7.43 train once again stops at Bexland for the convenience of myself and other passengers.

I look forward to a positive response.

Yours faithfully,

Diane Peterson

Task 2

Bringing up children is one of the most important things that people do and if both parents work it can be even more stressful and tiring. This is why some people advocate that governments should provide financial support so that at least one parent could stay at home with a very young child. This would have a number of advantages and disadvantages for individuals and society.

In some countries the government has introduced policies to encourage couples to have more children. Many parents would like to stay home to look after their very young children, but cannot survive on just one income. If parents were paid by the government, this would probably lead to an increase in the birth rate, which would benefit society as a whole.

It would also be to the advantage of the infant because it could have more contact with its mother or father at a very important stage in its life. The parent who was at home full-time would be able to develop a stronger bond with his or her child.

One of the major drawbacks of such a policy would be its cost. Meeting this would require an increase in tax or a diversion of government funds from other purposes. Some people would object to subsidising the upbringing of other people's children. The amount of money paid and the length of time for which it was paid would be important considerations. In addition, many people believe that the world is already overpopulated and that governments should not encourage an increase in population.

Although there are a number of arguments to be made in favour of and against this idea, I feel that overall there is more to gain for both individuals and society from such a policy.

Writing Test 2

Sample responses

Task 1

Dear Jane,

Do you remember the apartment we were living in when you came to visit us a couple of years ago? Well, we felt that it was getting too small for us, or to be more exact, that our two kids had outgrown it and needed more space to run around. We spent about six months looking for a house and last month we finally moved into one we've bought.

It's a three-bedroom, older style brick house in Haverton, but one of the best things about it is that it's got a big yard and a garden, and it's in a quiet street. Plus it's got two bathrooms, which makes it easier when four people are getting ready for work and school in the mornings. It's such a contrast to the cramped place and noisy area we were in before.

It'd be great if you could come and visit us some time. We'd love to see you again – you could come for an evening meal or spend the whole day with us. Anyway, get in touch and let's see if we can make a time.

Best wishes,

Tim

Task 2

The media often carries stories on the adventures of individuals, including teenagers, engaging in physically very demanding activities such as climbing Mount Everest or sailing solo around the world. I don't think these kinds of feats are good models, because they are beyond the capacity of the average person. If tempted to try this kind of activity most people are more likely to risk being killed or badly injured, or being psychologically damaged due to failure, rather than gaining in courage and confidence.

Courage is not the same thing as risk-taking and confidence is distinct from being foolhardy; courage and confidence are characteristics that can be very useful in life as they help people go beyond their comfort zone and achieve worthwhile goals. However, true courage and confidence can be built up gradually through more mundane means, such as by facing the everyday problems that are part of being human,

and trying to find honest and moral ways of solving them.

In fact, individuals, particularly young people showing off or trying to prove themselves, often get into great danger when engaged in 'heroic', attention-grabbing leisure activities, and then a lot of money and time can be spent by other people who have to put their own lives at risk trying to save them.

If people want to do these kinds of leisure activities because they enjoy them and find them exciting, they should be free to do so provided that they do not harm others. People should be encouraged to do exercise because it is an essential ingredient for health, but there is no need to court danger. No one should feel under pressure to do something spectacular in the hope that it will make them a better person.

Writing Test 3

Sample responses

Task 1

Dear Sir/Madam,

My name is Bill Emery, the tenant renting your apartment in Halloran St. I am writing to you because I am planning to go abroad soon and would like to ask whether you would have any objection to a friend of mine staying in the apartment while I am away.

Next month I am going on a trip around Europe for about two months. I thought it would be good if someone could stay in the apartment while I am away. David Harper, who I have known since high school, is keen to move in while I am away. He is an honest and reliable person, and is sure to keep the place clean and tidy. He shares a house with three other people and would welcome the opportunity to be in a quiet place where he could get more study done.

I would appreciate it if you would give me permission to have David stay in the apartment while I am away. I would pay the rent in advance and of course I would be liable should any damage be caused in my absence.

Yours faithfully,

Bill Emery

NOTES

Following the conventions of letter-writing, this letter commences with a greeting (*Dear Sir/Madam,*) and ends with a formulation and signature (*Yours faithfully, Bill Emery*).

The tone is formal and polite, as it is asking for permission from a person who the writer has a lease with, and the letter is to the point.

In a formal letter such as this, full words have been used instead of contractions; for example, *I am* instead of *I'm* and *it would* instead of *it'd*.

The first paragraph sets out the purpose of the letter, the second gives details about the trip and the friend, and the third more formally asks permission.

All three bullet points are covered, and concrete information such as the destination of the trip and the name and character of the friend are given, and there is a promise to take responsibility.

There are 191 words.

Task 2

People's quality of life is generally enhanced by living with pets, and this applies for older people as well. Animals provide companionship, they can be interesting to observe, and looking after them can lead to people getting more exercise and taking better care of themselves. There are, however, situations when keeping a pet can endanger an older person's health.

As many senior citizens live alone, a pet can help reduce feelings of loneliness. A cat or dog communicates with and is affectionate towards its owner. Having a bond with an animal can give you a psychological boost and thus improve your physical health.

When humans have to look after a baby and provide it with attention, they tend to take better care of themselves. Pets can have the same effect on their owners. And as dogs need to be taken for walks, this leads to their owners getting some daily exercise too.

There are, on the other hand, situations in which pets can have a detrimental impact on their owners. The elderly can easily suffer broken bones if they have a fall, and it is very easy to be tripped up by a cat under your feet. Some people can develop allergies to cat fur or dog hair, or be infected by diseases that animals carry. And a home with a large number of cats, dogs or birds can quickly become unhygienic.

Humans enjoy and benefit from living with animals in a number of ways that make them healthier and improve their lives. Only in rare cases is the interaction between pets and humans not a positive one.

NOTES

In this essay the opening paragraph suggests the writer has a positive view, but also indicates possible problems. The following two paragraphs detail some benefits, while the fourth paragraph explains potential risks. The concluding paragraph sums up the argument.

A range of vocabulary is used, with *pets* also referred to as *animals* and *creatures*, *old people* as *older person*, *senior citizens* and *the elderly*, and *improved* is paraphrased as *enhanced*. There is also a variety of sentence structures.

There are 268 words.

Writing Test 4

Sample responses

Task 1

Dear Mary,

I thought I'd drop you a line to let you know what I've been up to since I left the clinic.

You remember I said I needed to have a change? Well, I got a job working part-time in a cafe not far from my place. I make coffee, take customers' orders, serve food and drinks, make sandwiches and do some cleaning up.

It's hectic at times in the cafe, but nowhere near as stressful as nursing work. I miss being able to help sick people and I'd prefer a nurse's wage, but I don't miss the unpaid overtime and masses of paperwork. Working part-time means that now I'm doing a lot of the things I enjoy that I didn't have the time or energy for before, so I really don't regret switching jobs. And anyway, if I really feel the urge I can go back to nursing one day.

And what about you? I'd love to have a long chat with you and the others. Perhaps we could have a meal one night after work. Hope to see you soon.

Yours,

Anne

NOTES

Following the conventions of letter-writing, this letter commences with a greeting (*Dear Mary,*) and ends with a formulation and signature (*Yours, Anne*).

The tone is conversational, informal and friendly (this is reflected in expressions such as *drop you a line, what I've been up to, masses of paperwork, a long chat*), as it is a letter from one person to a workmate who she seems to have got along well with.

In an informal letter such as this, some contractions have been used instead of full words; for example, *I'd* instead of *I would* and *don't* instead of *do not*. With this task, it would be possible to write in a more formal style to a former workmate or someone who you were not so close to, such as a former supervisor.

The first paragraph briefly explains the purpose of the letter, the second gives details about the new job, the third discusses whether changing jobs was a good decision, and the fourth suggests that they meet.

There are 185 words.

Task 2

Taxation is used to redistribute income between individuals and from individuals towards collective purposes, so it is unavoidable that there will be winners and losers.

High-income individuals who pay very high taxes may view such taxes as theft. If some of that money is given to individuals with low incomes as welfare payments, these poorer individuals would benefit.

Tax has been called the price of civilisation. People with high incomes can enjoy living in a safer society with a lower crime rate if the money taken from them in tax is used well and there is not a big gap between the rich and the poor.

The argument is often made that if taxes are too high, this will act as a brake on motivation and innovation, as wealthier people will not want to see the fruits of their labour taken by the state, and may be tempted to take their assets and ideas to another country where tax rates are lower. If this happened, the country with high tax rates would suffer.

The main beneficiary of a policy of very high taxes is the country as a whole, in other words, society. That money can be used to raise standards of health and education, as welfare payments for those in need, and to upgrade infrastructure. However, there are no guarantees. If taxes are spent wastefully or the money goes into the pockets of corrupt officials, then only those officials and their cronies reap the benefit, and at everyone else's cost.

Thus the effect of tax policy is not always what one might expect, and the overall impact on individuals and society depends on a range of other factors apart from the rate of tax.

SPEAKING
Sample speaking tests

The following is an analysis of the performance of the three candidates in the sample speaking test on pages 104–17.

Assessment of Candidate 1

Fluency and coherence

This candidate occasionally spoke fluently, but overall the pace was too slow and he hesitated frequently. Some pauses before answering were too long. His delivery was not smooth and far too often he filled pauses with 'er' while thinking of the next word he wanted to say. This was particularly noticeable during the long presentation in the second part of the test, but occurred throughout the interview. Using such fillers as a technique to gain thinking time is part of normal speech, but if overused, they disturb the flow of conversation. He did not use the full minute that candidates are given to prepare their long presentation, and started to speak after about 15 seconds. Due to his slow pace, and with the pauses and hesitations, during the long presentation he was not able to say very much. Overall, he made very few long utterances.

Throughout the interview he clearly understood and gave coherent answers to the questions, though there were a couple of exceptions. When asked 'How do people usually find a place to live in your country?', he answered, 'The people, er, find, a quiet place to live in my country because the centre is so crowded and so noisy'. On a number of occasions when he had not understood a question, he asked for it to be repeated, which is quite acceptable in the test. Repeating or rephrasing words used by the other person is a way to get thinking time, or to ask for clarification and maintain coherence. When asked about places that 'are more pleasant to live in', he simply and correctly asked 'More?' However, he seldom echoed or rephrased words from the questions, apart from when he was asked about 'other factors' and he responded, 'I think main factor is ...' He incorrectly echoed the examiner when he was asked 'what do you think are the healthiest drinks?' and he replied, 'I like healthiest drinks'.

Vocabulary

The candidate generally used vocabulary appropriately, but displayed only a limited range. On one of the few occasions when he used a less common word, it was used incorrectly: he talked of 'metropole cities' instead of 'metropolitan cities'. He said, 'my first degree is economy' instead of 'Economics', and 'I have to learn to economy news' instead of 'I have to keep up with news about the economy'. Particularly in giving information about himself, he should make sure that he uses the correct terminology.

Throughout the interview he used the word 'yeah', whereas 'yes' would be more appropriate for a formal speaking test. Some other examples of vocabulary used wrongly were when he referred to 'some celebrates' instead of 'celebrations' or when he said 'we have no residence areas', 'it has a high level of alcohol inside' instead of 'it contains a high level of alcohol', 'go by walking' instead of 'go on foot' or 'walk', 'we have a good relation in our apartments' (though later he correctly mentions 'relationships') and 'I can see a ocean or river or like this, or lake' instead of 'or something like this, or a lake'. He used 'very', 'little' and 'quite' as qualifiers, but said 'it's too different' instead of it's very different'.

Grammar

It is generally possible to understand what this candidate meant throughout the interview, even when he made errors, and there were many instances of grammar being used correctly. In some cases he corrected himself, for instance: 'and it's, er, it has, our home, flat has three rooms', 'you must', er, moving, eh you can be moved'. However, there were very few complex sentences and, as with vocabulary, there was an insufficient range of grammatical structures.

The simple present tense was almost the only tense used. On a few occasions he left out 'are', ('gossip magazines popular in my country', 'the people interested in this gossip or sport'), or else used 'is' instead of 'are' with a plural noun ('in my country is most popular drinks special Turkish drinks', 'the people is elite people', 'our home prices is not, er, high'). He generally used the final -s when necessary except when he said, 'my mum actually like the huge kitchen'. He also used the wrong verb: 'I don't interested gossip'. In one case the continuous form was used instead of the simple present: 'we talking to neighbours always' and the simple instead of the continuous: 'That's why I study English'. When it was necessary to use the simple past passive, it was done incorrectly: 'this building, this apartments, er, built several years ago'. On two occasions the -ing form was used instead of the infinitive: 'if you rent a house you can, er, you must, er, moving', 'prefer to buying a home'.

The plural forms of nouns were generally used correctly, but there were some exceptions: 'lots of facility', 'in Istanbul the people generally live in the apartment', 'there are lots of advantage or disadvantage', 'our neighbours also is kind peoples'. There were cases where the wrong preposition was used ('IT is related about information', 'this apartment's a little

far to centre', 'this is other factor for choose their apartment', 'when I look at [out] the window'), or a preposition was used where it was not needed ('that's why the people prefer to magazines', 'the people prefer to quiet place'), or where the preposition was omitted ('the disadvantages own the house', 'always you live the same place').

Articles were mostly used correctly, but sometimes they were omitted: 'we lived in, er, seventh floor', 'I think main factor is, er, their jobs', 'it's advantage for make a good relationships'. Also, a couple of pronouns were omitted: 'I don't read [them] often', 'people prefer to drink [it]'.

Among other grammatical errors, there was one example of an incomplete comparative ('high quality than the others'); incorrect word order with adverbs ('you can get easily a friend', 'you can get easily a home'); the wrong word order with adjectives ('I, er, wants to live a, er, good view, has a good view apartments'); and an error in use of the negative ('if you live in the houses, er, you have, er, not a good relationships there for their neighbours').

Pronunciation

Generally, this candidate's pronunciation was clear, though it would have helped if he spoke a bit more loudly so that the listener did not need to strain to understand him. There were problems with some sounds (e.g. 'th'), and some words (e.g. 'metropole cities' and 'huge'). Word and sentence stress was good, as was linking (e.g. 'has a high level of alcohol inside', 'if you rent a house, you can'), although the overuse of fillers disrupted the linking of words. The slow pace, pauses and the frequent use of 'er' produced an uneven rhythm of speech.

Overall

The level of this candidate's spoken English is not yet high enough for study at university in an English-speaking country. He is relaxed, perhaps too relaxed, and needs to make his delivery smoother, faster, more coherent and more accurate. His level of self-correction makes him hard to understand and affects his fluency, coherence and accuracy. He needs to work on his accuracy in order to reduce this level of self-correction, and thereby improve his fluency. It would be useful for him to listen to many types of spoken English and to engage in conversation on a range of topics with different people.

Assessment of Candidate 2

Fluency and coherence

This candidate always responded appropriately and promptly, giving detailed answers and engaging well with the examiner throughout, creating the impression from the beginning of the interview that she was speaking fluently. She was forthcoming and produced a lot of long utterances. When asked 'Why did you decide to do a Masters of Commerce?', she answered, 'Um, because I think, if I can gain the Master degree maybe I will give a good job in China. And I will have a more opportunity to get a good pay job which is more appealing'. When asked 'What are the most popular drinks in your country?', she answered, 'Beer, yeah … And, er, maybe Coca-Cola, but I dislike it. I always drink the orangey water and, uh, just drink the water'. Unlike the male candidate, she used the full minute to prepare her long presentation, and spoke more coherently and logically in that section of the test.

She made good use of words and expressions such as 'however' and 'of course'. When she did not understand a question, she asked 'Sorry?' or else repeated the word the examiner had used which she had not understood: 'Toward?', 'Treat?' She also established coherence by rephrasing words used by the examiner. When asked 'What factors do you think determine where people choose to live?', she said, 'I think most of … most of the important reason'. On a couple of occasions she did not answer the question, such as her incoherent response when asked about healthy drinks.

Vocabulary

In general, the vocabulary and expressions she used were appropriate although she lacked some basic vocabulary (for example, she used 'parking room' for 'garage'). However, her vocabulary range is often quite limited. She confused 'few' and 'little' when she said 'I have little friend', and several times used adjectives instead of nouns ('the important reason is comfortable and the price and the convenient') and nouns instead of adjectives ('the life is very leisure'). She is clearly a person who likes to communicate and was able to paraphrase to express what she wanted to say, though she rarely used idioms and the only less common expression she used was 'in a word'. She needs to find alternative ways to say 'I think' to express her opinions and to use more qualifiers than 'very' and 'quite'. Overall the range and level of vocabulary was simple.

Grammar

This candidate made a lot of basic errors, particularly with verb tenses and the use of the plural. Students with her level of English usually have studied the rules of the English tense system, but have problems using verbs correctly. She was generally good with the third person singular, yet often mixed confused tenses: 'I will going to have the Master of Commerce', 'If I have rent a house and I lived it for a, for a long time maybe I think oh it's OK to me, but when I look, um, with it to my friend maybe I will find out that his house is better to me, so I will all think maybe I will have to looking for another house'. She sometimes used the wrong verbs: 'I have the language courses in my college', 'the house has in Willoughby'. She needs to use the simple past tense more often: 'when I first came to Sydney' instead of 'once I have been to Sydney', and 'when I in China I live in the apartment'. The -ing form was sometimes omitted or misused: 'I will not spend a lot of time to see the magazine', 'instead of go outside', 'want to looking for a house'. She had trouble using conditional, hypothetical structures: 'If I have my own house I lived in it and I feel oh that it, that belongs to me. And I think I have a family, um, but if I live in the house just rent from somebody, I think I'm always worried'. However, she did better later in the interview: 'If you want to go out or go to work, go to university, you'll find that the traffic always block, it will waste a lot of time'.

She often used the singular form of nouns rather than plurals: 'magazine', 'movie star, TV star and the singer, the famous singer', 'one of the reason', 'six bedroom', 'one of the problem', 'sometime they can find the insect climbing to my house. I'm afraid of it'.

But sometimes she used plurals correctly: 'and in other big cities'. As often happens with people whose first language does not use articles, she sometimes used them when they were not necessary: 'a lot of younger people like to see the magazine about it'.

The pronoun object was left out at times. When asked 'Are there any hot drinks you like?', she replied: 'No I don't like'; also 'they cannot control'. Some errors were also made with prepositions: 'study is better to me', 'not good enough to me' and the very common error 'most of people'.

She was quick to correct herself, such as when she said, 'such as beer or alcohol, alcohol water. Yeah alcohol drink, sorry'. In fact, she should have used the adjective 'alcoholic', but she was clearly monitoring her own words. Overall she showed a limited range of grammatical structures, though her errors seldom led to the listener misunderstanding what she meant.

Pronunciation

This candidate spoke in a loud, clear voice throughout the interview. There were mispronunciations, especially of sounds that are typically difficult for speakers of her first language, such as 'Macquarie'. She had difficulty with the pronunciation of some high-frequency words and expressions such as 'good pay job', 'college', 'which', 'high' and 'chat'. Often she linked sounds well, as with: 'I will continue my studies throughout my life' and 'it's very easy for you to go out for shopping'. She stressed the important words in sentences: 'maybe I will give a good job in China', 'maybe the *environment* is not good enough'. Yet she needs to use more weak forms. In some utterances, each word was given equal stress: 'you can gain some information about the magazine', 'but I dislike it', 'when I live in it' and 'most of people prefer to live in his own house because the rent of the house is quite expensive'. Her intonation is influenced by her native language, and although at times she uses stress timing and intonation to good effect, overall she uses non-standard intonation patterns that affect how she conveys meaning.

Overall

This candidate is an effective speaker but her spoken English level is not adequate for university level study. Although she seems quite fluent, her vocabulary range is limited to basic words and phrases, and her control of accurate grammatical structures is weak. Outside familiar topics she begins to lose the precision to explain what she really means. She needs to improve her accuracy, to expand her vocabulary into more precise terms that better express her meaning, and to use sentence stress and intonation more effectively. She may benefit by slightly slowing down the pace of her delivery to give a more considered response.

Assessment of Candidate 3

Fluency and coherence

As a fluent communicator, this candidate readily and confidently answers questions and expresses opinions, and generally responds appropriately and at length. He occasionally corrects himself, which is common in spoken language and quite acceptable in the test. There are few hesitations and they are mostly not long. If anything, the pace was too fast and speech would be more coherent if he spoke more slowly. Though he did make full use of the minute to prepare his long presentation, he would benefit from taking more time to think about what he is going to say.

His speech is generally coherent, though this does break down at times, particularly with a tendency to overuse some connectives, and to sometimes use them inappropriately. This can be seen especially with his use of the word 'so' at the beginning of utterances. For example, when asked which kinds of magazines are popular in his country, he responds, 'So in India people love cricket so the ...' and in the long turn when he says, 'So I love gardening also so I had a lot of flowers and er whether you sit at my place some home gardens. So the house was my favourite house in my whole life er until now. So I am still looking for a house for that kind of house. So because I want to live in a very peaceful area ...'. He also overuses 'also' when he says, 'they can use the internet also, it is really helpful. So you can do it at home also you don't have to go and see someone else so you can find it very easily on the internet also'. There is also a tendency to overuse the filler 'like', which is commonly used in informal language: 'Er in books like people have to spend a lot of time to get a idea what they reading about but in magazines they can get like er, er they can get an idea about the thing what they are reading about just in a shorter um period, short period of time and in a sense like short look, quick look, yeah.'

In addition, he overuses the conjunction 'and', for example, 'so these people are really helpful and they can find whatever they are looking for that's easy for them because they can tell them those people like what they are looking for and they will help to find those places and even on the other hand they can use the internet also, it is really helpful. So you can do it at home also you don't have to go and see someone else ...'. On occasion what he is referring to is unclear, for instance when he says, 'I want to do that nursing course' and 'it tells about those other products'.

Vocabulary

This candidate's range of vocabulary is adequate to convey what he wants to say, and he uses a number of idiomatic and less common lexical items appropriately. Examples are when he says, 'I'm really into like um looking after people', 'veggies', and with collocations such as 'homemade alcohol', 'separate toilet', 'dark chocolate' and 'basic needs'. He appears to be more comfortable in the use of less formal language (exceptions are when he says 'dispensaries' and 'congested').

In general his vocabulary lacks flexibility and precision, and he has a limited capacity to paraphrase. He makes some inappropriate choices when he says 'street view' instead of 'view of the street', 'migrant peoples' instead of 'migrants', 'colour wise and picture wise and the furniture wise', and 'line of poverty'. There is sometimes confusion between adjectives, nouns and adverbs e.g. 'the government financial', 'when I firstly came to Australia', and 'suburban is more wider than city'.

Grammar

This candidate produces complex sentences, though these frequently contain errors, e.g. 'if you are living in a house you have a separate wall from your neighbours or you will have a gap between your house and the neighbour's house, so you can't hear the neighbour's cry so it will be more separate from the – from other houses' ... and 'in some like in developing countries the government should help those people who can't afford to buy a place um like um mostly those people who are living below the line, the line of poverty, so government should help them to buy a place'. There are also numerous errors with basic grammar, including with articles, tenses and prepositions.

Often the wrong tense is used, for instance when describing a place where he used to live he says, 'I like that because there is a park on the next side of the street. So I can watch people playing football because I love football and er it was near to all the facilities'. Also there are errors with the form of tenses, e.g. 'what they reading about' and ' you kind of feeling like'. This is also lack of agreement between subject and verb e.g. 'people who er owns their own home' and 'the curtains was really nice'.

There are numerous instances of errors in the use of comparatives e.g. 'more bigger than a apartment', 'more taller than a house ', 'some residential areas are very like er very good than others' and 'these kinds of places are very comfortable than others'. There are errors with articles, particularly omitting them: 'it's not interesting subject', 'get a idea' and 'view of city'. The incorrect preposition is sometimes used e.g. 'near to', 'there is a park on the next side of the street' and 'on the wedding parties'.

Though what this candidate means is generally clear, there are several occasions when it is difficult to understand what he is trying to say. Instances of this are when he says, 'because uh in in this competition of us uh you need English if you are going it helps in your career', ' a house would be like very open side' and ' suburban is more wider than city'.

Pronunciation

Most of the time this candidate can be understood, yet his pronunciation would improve if he spoke more slowly. The main problems are at the level of sentences and phrases, where his intonation and rhythm sometimes make his message hard to comprehend, rather than with individual words. Meaning can be conveyed or made clearer through using pauses, yet there are insufficient pauses in this candidate's rapid-fire speech, and it is at times not immediately clear when he has finished responding to a question, e.g. due to him not using falling intonation.

Words are sometimes run together and the lack of chunking makes it difficult to tell when one idea has ended and another has begun. Some individual words and expressions are hard to understand, particularly due to a tendency to make long vowels into short vowels and through the wrong stress within words, e.g. with 'communicate', 'players', 'magazines', 'look', 'alcohol', 'peaceful', 'street', 'library', 'colour' and 'developing'.

Overall

Some people speak too slowly in the attempt to avoid errors and some have the opposite tendency. That is, they are so keen to communicate that they do not take enough care with accuracy. This candidate seems to belong to the latter group. He is adept at using colloquial vocabulary and has the confidence to communicate fluently, even if he sometimes lacks coherence. Overall, if he slowed down the pace at which he talks, he would have more time to think, which would mean he would not have to correct himself and change direction midway through sentences so often. This would also help him avoid some of the grammar mistakes, enable him to produce more coherent utterances, to use words such as 'yeah', 'so' and 'like' less often, and he would be easier to understand.

Audio CD contents